M000188060

Sports Bar

BRYAN PAIEMENT

COCKTAILS AND SPORTS TRIVIA

RED ⚡ LIGHTNING BOOKS

This book is a publication of

Red Lightning Books
1320 East 10th Street
Bloomington, Indiana 47405 USA

redlightningbooks.com

This book is printed on acid-free paper.

Manufactured in China

First printing 2021

ISBN 978-1-68435-175-6 (hdbk.)
ISBN 978-1-68435-176-3 (web PDF)

All cocktail images courtesy of Sky Pond
Photography & Video Productions, Inc.

A toast to my parents, Pierre and Paula, and their unwavering support and encouragement.

CONTENTS

FOREWORD

In many uncelebrated ways, sports is a world of lobbies.

Jim Valvano, the late, great basketball humorist/coach, first stumbled upon that notion some years back. He was sitting in a lobby somewhere when he realized how central lobbies are to sports. Regardless of the event—hockey's Stanley Cup, college basketball's Final Four, the Super Bowl of the NFL, name your favorite happening—the hotel lobby provides sanctuary for that odd collection of people who follow the games. Fans, former players, broadcasters, writers, analysts, young statisticians, old coaches, equipment salespeople—they all find their way to the barstools and couches, where they kibitz until the wee hours, re-playing contests, advancing and testing theorems, trading tales and gossip, and talking up the game: what was, what might have been, what will be.

They smoke; they dream; they commune with the great spirits of sport. You'd be hard-pressed to find one of them with-out a drink in hand. And I am one of them, a deep sub on life's all-lobby team.

That's why I've been so delighted by Bryan Paiement's book of cocktails. I can open it and dream about all sorts of elixirs, the more exotic, the better. Whether your space is the lobby of the team hotel or your special tailgate or even the privacy of your man or woman cave, you have to know the playbook. And this sweet little volume is it.

And it's even more important for those days when you don't have any big games at all. It's then that you can thumb through the pages and dream and experiment to get ready to put your game face on.

Here's to the mix. Cheers!

Roland Lazenby
Author of *Michael Jordan, The Life*

ACKNOWLEDGMENTS

A huge thank-you to my wife, Dana, whose willingness to imbibe, taste testing a multitude of cocktails, no matter how unorthodox the ingredients, helped to shape the finished product. Tasting cocktails is a tall task to ask of anyone, but someone has to do it!

A special thank-you to Alex Ho, owner of Sky Pond Photography and Video Productions in Estes Park, Colorado. The *Sports Bar* project would not have been possible without his expertise and artistic eye in framing the cocktail photos.

Thank you to renowned author Roland Lazenby for lending his words to the project and helping to enhance *Sports Bar*.

And a huge thank-you to my agent, Joseph Perry, whose hard work helped make *Sports Bar* possible.

Pregame Introduction

I know you're itching to get to the game, so thank you for taking the time to read a bit about what's in store for you in *Sports Bar: Cocktails and Sports Trivia*. If you were like me growing up, then you may be somewhat sad that you're not actually a professional athlete at this point in your life and the sporting events in this book don't include inside information about you, the pro athlete. I loved playing sports as a kid—and still do. I'm a decent athlete, so naturally as a kid I figured I'd be making outrageous sums of money and living the life of an adored athlete as an adult. But, hey, I'm not, and odds are you aren't either, so rather than stew on our "change of life course" from when we were younger, let's bask in it and celebrate the athletes who make their incredibly rare talents look effortless.

As I mentioned above, I love watching, playing, and talking sports. Working as a professional bartender at a resort in Estes Park, Colorado, affords me the opportunity to watch every major event and talk shop accordingly. The beautiful thing about living in a small destination town just outside Rocky Mountain National Park is the diversity the mountains attract every summer; people from the opposite side of the country, the opposite side of the world, take the time to take a seat at the bar, and, inspired by the whatever sporting event may be taking place, a conversation is sparked. It's these conversations about sports and the often unbelievable and fascinating facts I learn from these patrons that gave me the idea to put together a book that melds my two passions: booze and sports.

As a bartender, I have the opportunity to be creative and create drink specials inspired by different sports throughout the year. In April, the Masters takes place at Augusta National, a golf tournament—*the* golf tournament—that deserves its own cocktail, which became Augusta on My Mind. The cocktail utilizes the highlights and backstory of the Masters and golf in general: blended scotch from Scotland, where the game was invented; hibiscus simple syrup to pay homage to the pristine flora flanking the course; and grapefruit juice to add just the right amount of pink to resemble the azaleas the tournament is so famous for. I find that watching these amazing competitions throughout the year is just more fun when an inspired cocktail accompanies them. We're going to imbibe while watching anyway, so why not have a delicious libation to sip?

So, what if you're not a big sports fan? Should this book be destined just to be a wedge for your lopsided table? A regift item for that uncle who won't shut up about sports? The simple answer is no! The cocktails in *Sports Bar* can easily stand alone without the aid of a game or tournament. However, I urge you sports haters out there to whip up the cocktail and then discuss some of the remarkable sports trivia with those around. For instance, did you know that the number of vasectomy procedures performed on men increases exponentially in advance of March Madness? It seems men are much more willing to go through with the procedure knowing they'll be able to sit on a frozen donut for a week and watch the tournament guilt-free. Ladies, let's see what else we'll do, especially when the Stanley Cup Finals are on!

I've read through many cocktail books with delicious drinks. Yet obscure, hard-to-find ingredients act only to deter the reader from actually making the cocktail. Relax—all the ingredients and directions for making the drinks in this book are very straightforward, the ingredients readily available at your local liquor store. No online ordering necessary.

I had a great time creating *Sports Bar*—not only did I learn incredible facts researching my favorite sports events, but I was able to play the part of "mad mixologist" in the kitchen, working and reworking drink concoctions until I got them just right. I can't tell you how many times after shaking cocktails for a fourth or fifth time in a night, I had to reassure my wife that this was part of my book project, my "research."

We're fortunate to live in a world where you can blindly pick any date on the calendar and there's a great sporting event to watch. In completing this project, I was astounded by how much of our conversation, both social and at work, revolves around the combination of imbibing and sports—perhaps the World's Greatest Combo.

1
𝓢porting 𝓖oods

Shaker The shaker is by far the most important piece of equipment you will need to create the cocktails in *Sports Bar*. I prefer the Boston shaker, which is a two-piece shaker and a Hawthorne strainer. Of course, you can use the Cobbler shaker with the built-in strainer if you prefer. Also, a julep strainer is a nice tool to have to strain stirred drinks from a mixing glass that don't need to be shaken.

Jigger Measuring your liquid ingredients is crucial to any properly mixed cocktail. You could invest in speed pourers and work on your free pour using a count in your head, or you could just buy a metal hourglass jigger with a 1 ½ ounce measurement on one end and ¾ ounce on the other. (I would definitely go the jigger route.)

Strainer I love to use fresh ingredients—especially fresh fruit—in cocktails. Freshness is the difference between a so-so cocktail and a delicious one. When you start muddling fruit and herbs, there's bound to be small bits left over in the mixing glass that you don't want in the cocktail—this is where a small, cone-shaped, fine-mesh strainer, or double strainer, as it's called, comes in handy. Simply strain your cocktail through the Hawthorne strainer while holding the second cup strainer over the drink—this should eliminate all the bits that might otherwise float in your drink.

Muddler This is maybe the cheapest, easiest-to-find piece of equipment for your home bar. The muddler serves as the Presser, the releaser of all oils, juices, and fragrances that will serve as the base for many of your cocktails.

Channel knife (or vegetable peeler) To get the great-looking garnishes—your fun twists and peels that complete the cocktails—you'll need your channel knife. Again, this is an easy tool to find in most stores.

Paring knife The paring knife is key for making those fun, fancy garnishes like lemon twists, spirals, and wedges. Really, any shape garnish you need can be made by cutting and then trimming the peel off of whatever citrus, herb, or fruit you wish to use. This is a great tool for finishing off your cocktails and impressing your friends with your presentation skills.

Hand juicer I always use a handheld juicer that works very well to extract the deliciousness from fruits; simply cut the fruit horizontally and press. The handheld juicers come in a variety of sizes, so choose whatever works best for you. Of course, larger fruits can be cut into smaller pieces to fit your juicer.

Glassware My wife will tell you what a fan I am of glassware. I love searching for unique pieces that will work for cocktails, but there are definitely a few staple glasses you should have in your cabinet: a martini or coupe glass, wine and champagne glasses, Collins glass, and rocks and highball glasses—the essentials, but don't be timid to add more and more glassware.

Ice molds I have a few different ice molds, and this is an area of mixology where you can get creative and play around with different forms. I would suggest having at least two standard molds—the round ice mold and the square. Not only will they make your cocktail look polished and impress your friends, but they melt much slower than average ice cubes and won't dilute your drink as quickly.

2
Batching Cocktails

Sports' greatest achievement may be that of the Great Con-
gregator since no other activity on earth has the ability to bring
millions upon millions of people together from all walks of life
to enjoy a singular event. It's an amazing spectacle really. I love
hosting friends and family and whipping up cocktails for everyone to enjoy, especially when there's a great game to watch.
When batching cocktails, there's really no one *right* way to do
it—it's all a matter of preference and taste. That being said, water
must somehow find its way into your cocktails—not only does
the H_2O help chill your cocktails when you shake a drink with
ice, but it also provides a necessary dilution of your drink so
you're not sipping on a libation with the strength to kill a small
bull.

In general, your cocktails should have around 20–25 percent water whether you are shaking them individually or batching for a group. I've found the most precise method for me is to
measure the contents of a drink pre-ice, then shake with ice and
remeasure to find exactly how much water was incorporated after shaking the cocktail. For example, the sidecar cocktail starts
with 2 ounces of brandy, 1 ounce of Cointreau, and ¾ ounce of
fresh lemon juice. So, my base for this drink is 3 ¾ ounces. Next,
I'll shake the drink with ice, then remeasure to find my new total
ounce measurement. Let's say an additional ounce was added, so
now I know if I'm making a batch of cocktails for twelve people,
I'll add 12 ounces of water to the pitcher (on top of my original
measurements, which were also multiplied by 12). When making cocktails with citrus, I tend to pull back on the juice because
when scaled up, citrus juice can be overpowering. Hosting a party and batching cocktails can get pricey, so it's always smart to

leave yourself the option of adding citrus to taste to avoid having to toss out an entire pitcher because it's too tart to enjoy.

It's important to remember to hold off on adding the citrus to your batch until you're ready to serve because it doesn't do well sitting long. Also, when batching cocktails with bitters, do not automatically scale up according to the number of your guests. Bitters are powerful, and it's always a good idea to start with about half of the amount you would use if you were to scale accordingly. For instance, the Manhattan typically has two dashes of Angostura bitters per cocktail, so if you need to batch for a group of eight, you would start with half of the typical amount needed and add eight dashes of bitters instead of sixteen. You can always add more bitters, but you can't take them out.

Another method for batching is simply to change the ounces in your recipe to cups, which will render you eight servings of your cocktail. Again, with bitters and citrus, you have to be careful not to scale up in exact relation to your other ingredients because they will overpower your cocktail and leave your guests begging for beer instead. Once you have changed the measurement over to cups, you can add 20–25 percent water, which will help to chill and dilute your cocktail for optimal sipping pleasure. Batching is often a matter of trial and error, and everyone's preferences and tastes are different, but these two methods have served me, and my guests, well.

3
Golf

THE MASTERS

The Masters: the greatest tournament in golf, hands down. The hallowed grounds at Augusta National Golf Club have produced an array of memorable moments: Tiger's demolishing of the field by twelve strokes in 1997, Mickelson's eighteen-footer to earn him his first Masters (and first-ever major), and Tiger's unbelievable chip shot on Hole 16, just to name a few. The definitive golf tournament deserves a delicious cocktail, which is where Augusta on My Mind comes in. I use scotch as the base spirit, as Scotland is the land where golf was invented around 1457. The grapefruit and hibiscus simple syrup give the cocktail a nice pink color similar to the lush azaleas that are seen all over Augusta National Golf Course.

Augusta on My Mind

1 ½ oz. Dewar's Blended Scotch Whisky
2 oz. fresh squeezed grapefruit juice
¾ oz. hibiscus simple syrup*
2 rosemary sprigs (divided)

*Hibiscus simple syrup   Combine 1 cup granulated sugar with 1 cup water in a saucepan over medium heat. Stir frequently until sugar has been completely dissolved. Add 1 cup dried hibiscus flowers to the mixture, remove pan from heat, and let steep until flavor has been incorporated (thirty minutes to an hour).

<u>Here's How</u>   In a mixing glass, muddle rosemary, then add the grapefruit juice, syrup, and scotch. Add ice to mixing glass and

shake. Strain into a rocks glass with one large cube and garnish with rosemary sprig. Express (twist) grapefruit peel over the drink to release the peel's oil and slide the peel along the rim of the glass before rolling and adding as garnish on cocktail spear. Garnish with remaining rosemary sprig.

𝓗𝓸𝔀 '𝓑𝓸𝓾𝓽 𝓣𝓱𝓪𝓽!

• It's every professional golfer's dream and every ten-year-old child's nightmare: to put on the most coveted sports coat in golf, the green jacket. The iconic jacket was not always meant to be awarded to the winner of the Masters but rather for ushers to wear at the event to be easily located by attendees. Members of the club would wear the green jacket as a golf beacon of sorts in case those watching the tournament had questions. It wasn't until 1937 when the players began wearing the jackets as a fashion trophy. The Masters champion gets to hang on to the jacket for a year before it's returned to the club. They do get to permanently keep another green jacket that's tailor-made for them.

• The golf majors switch venues each year, except the Masters, which is held at Augusta National Golf Course every year.

• It hasn't always been roses and azaleas. Augusta National was founded at the beginning of the Great Depression, followed by World War II. Times were so tough, in fact, that the club didn't have the funds to pay the first winner of the Masters, Horton Smith, who captured the title in 1934. No top finishers were paid until about seventeen club members agreed to pitch in for the prize. Apparently, not everyone was in a "golfin' kinda mood," what with the Great Depression and all, and membership to Augusta National floundered: they only accrued 74 paying members instead of the 1,800 they'd been counting on.

- Augusta National was not always used as a playground for showcasing golf's greatest talents. Believe it or not, wartime had the audacity to interrupt tee times, and in 1942, Augusta National was turned into a livestock ranch with more than 200 cattle and 1,400 turkeys, a project designed to help the World War II effort, yet the project barely broke even. Next on the tee!—the golf course was reopened in 1944.

- Cub roar: In 1997, at the age of twenty-one years, three months, and fourteen days, Tiger Woods was the youngest player to win a Masters Tournament.

- A toast on Tuesday: Every Tuesday of Masters week, the defending champion of the tournament hosts the Champions Dinner—this is exclusive dining at its finest, and only past winners and club members are invited to participate.

- The Masters Tournament has something for everyone. Who cares if you don't enjoy watching or even playing golf? So what if you're bored to tears by the monotone golf announcers and repetitive swings? Just look at all the flowers! Every hole is named after the shrub or plant that adorns it. For example, Hole 2 is called Pink Dogwood because—yep, you guessed it—you'll find plenty of dogwoods flanking the fairway. An estimated eighty thousand plants have been added since the course was built.

- Master-ful firsts: The Masters was the first tournament to be featured nationwide on the radio and to use bleachers. Also, it was the first to use rope galleries and private detectives to handle ticket sales and security. Another great innovation credited to the Masters is the on-course scoreboard and the first use of the over/under par system, which was permanently put into place partly for those watching on black-and-white televisions who could not differentiate between scores that were shown in green and red.

- It's no secret that caddies carry yardage books for their players to measure different distances on the course to the hole, including odd spots like from benches or sprinkler heads. The books also contain odd numbers and letters, such as ICYFU: 221 or ICYRFU: 179. These cryptic codes stand for "In Case You Fuck Up" or "In Case You Really Fuck Up." I would have to add more self-deprecating acronyms to my yardage book, such as "WAYEPTDG: 234"—"Why Are You Even Playing This Damn Game?"

- A Bear of a record: Jack Nicklaus holds the record for most Masters wins with six. And just to prove his merit—as if he really had anything left to prove—Jack became the oldest player to win the Masters at forty-six years old in 1986.

US OPEN

The US Open is arguably the most difficult major to win in golf. Big-time names in the world of golf—Greg Norman, Nick Faldo, Phil Mickelson, Sam Snead—all have failed when it came to bringing home the US Open Championship Trophy. The trophy is the only major trophy not known by name, such as the Claret Jug for the Open or the Wanamaker Trophy for the Professional Golfers Association (PGA) Championship. It's reward enough to win the thing, forget all the silly names. In terms of venues that host the tournament that has lifted so many careers and broken the hearts of others, no one has played host to the US Open more than Oakmont Country Club in Pennsylvania. Oakmont, with its deep church pew bunkers and sloping greens, has hosted the event nine times and is regarded as one of the most difficult courses in North America. Oakmont It Is is a tribute to the US Open and Oakmont and uses the oaky and rich butter flavor of a lush Chardonnay as a base for the cocktail.

Oakmont It Is

4 oz. chardonnay
½ oz. lavender gin
2 oz. fresh squeezed orange juice
½ oz. simple syrup
3 rosemary sprigs (divided)
Orange wheels (garnish)
Club soda

<u>Here's How</u> In a mixing glass, muddle two rosemary sprigs to release the herb's oils. Add all remaining ingredients except club soda. Shake with ice and strain into a stemless wineglass filled three-quarters full of ice. Add club soda and give a quick stir. Garnish with orange wheels (in drink) and rosemary.

How 'Bout That!

- The 1912 US Open, held at the Country Club of Buffalo, was the first and only Open course to feature a par 6.
- Oakmont Country Club in Pittsburgh, Pennsylvania, has been the site of more US Opens than any other course. The 2007 US Open was the eighth time it was held there, and it was the site of the 2016 US Open.
- Swedish star Annika Sörenstam was the back-to-back US Women's Open Champion in 1995 and 1996 and is regarded as one of the greatest female golfers in the history of the game. In 1991, while playing at the University of Arizona, Sörenstam became the first foreign-born player to win the NCAA individual title and the first freshman winner.
- Apply overseas! International participants could qualify without coming to the United States starting with the 2005 US Open via tournaments held in England and Japan.
- The US Open invites professional or amateur golfers with a United States Golf Association (USGA) Handicap In-

dex not exceeding 1.4. I missed the cut by just twenty strokes ... on a good day.

• The first US Open was pushed back one month because of a scheduling conflict with the America's Cup yacht race. Held on October 4, 1895, at a nine-hole course at Newport Golf Club, the competition featured a field of ten professionals and one amateur who contended for the title over thirty-six holes in one day.

• Sinking his teeth in: Tiger Woods holds the record for the largest margin of victory at the US Open by winning by fifteen strokes in 2000.

• Five golfers have won all four majors, though none have done it in the same year: Ben Hogan, Gene Sarazen, Gary Player, Jack Nicklaus, and Tiger Woods.

• According to legend, on the last hole of the last round of the 1969 US Open, a marshal yelled at Orville Moody to "get behind the ropes," thinking he was a spectator. In fact, Moody was leading the tournament and would go on to capture his only PGA Tour win.

• Up a creek unfortunately with a club: The worst single hole score in a US Open belongs to Ray Ainsley in 1938. The trouble began when he hit his ball into the creek on the par-4 sixteenth at Cherry Hills Country Club. He kept swinging while his ball floated down the stream, and by the time his ball made it in the hole, he had posted a demoralizing 19.

• In 2002, the US Open was played at a publicly owned course for the first time, Bethpage State Park's Black Course in Farmingdale, New York.

• The 1974 US Open played host to the "Massacre at Winged Foot," which inspired one of the most famous US Open quotes of all time. With a struggling field (no one would break par; champion Hale Irwin finished 7-over 287), USGA Competition Committee chairman Sandy Tatum was forced to defend the course setup: "We're not trying to humiliate the best players in the world. We're simply trying to identify them." A fantastic summary of US Open play.

- International dominance . . . at first: There were sixteen consecutive international champions from the US Open's inception in 1895 to 1910, until John McDermott became the first American winner at the age of nineteen in 1911—still the youngest champion to this day.

- On account of Hinkle: The addition of the "Hinkle Tree" on the eighth fairway at Inverness Club in 1979 is the only major course redesign to happen during competitive play at the US Open. On the eighth hole, a par 5, Lon Hinkle used a gap in the trees to play onto the seventeenth fairway, which led to a birdie and encouraged his playing partner, Chi-Chi Rodríguez, to do the same and dramatically shorten the length of the par-5 eighth. A fifteen-foot tree was planted to close the gap after the first round, after dark, to prevent further "shortening of the hole."

The Ryder Cup

If you've had the pleasure of watching the Ryder Cup on TV or are one of the fortunate ones to have seen it in person, you understand the intensity and passion the golfers bring to the table, even when there's no money awarded. That's right: nations battle every two years for bragging rights and the pride of representing their country on the links. In the spirit of this competition, I created a drink that highlights a few of the finer things Europe and the United States have contributed to the world: bourbon, our fine state of Kentucky's greatest feat, and tea, the second-most-consumed drink in the world, only behind water.

Stroke of Nations

2 oz. Buffalo Trace Bourbon
1 ½ oz. chamomile tea
¼ oz. simple syrup
¼ oz. lemon juice
Anjou pear (1 quarter, muddled)

<u>Here's How</u> Muddle the pear in a mixing glass. Add ice and remaining ingredients and shake. Strain into a coupe glass. Garnish with pear slice.

How 'Bout That!

• Seeds of a great rivalry: In 1921, a match between the United States and Great Britain was promoted by the circulator manager of *Golf Illustrated*. Meanwhile, a British entrepreneur by the name of Samuel Ryder ran a number of golf tournaments with the goal of promoting his seed company. Ryder suffered from health problems, and his doctor gave him the most glorious doctor's note of all time: fresh air and regular exercise, in turn, golf, a prescription that was likely highly contested by his wife. Abe Mitchell, British golf legend, was hired by Ryder to teach him the skills of the trade. After watching Great Britain defeat the United States in an unofficial match, Ryder offered to donate a cup, and in 1927, the official Ryder Cup was born.

• Nasty mail: Injured players get the "special treatment" at the Ryder Cup; that is, the Ryder Cup captain puts their name in an envelope before the match begins. The opposing captain, be it for Europe or the United States, also must select a player from their team that they wish not to compete. The physically injured player and now emotionally injured player from the opposing side are matched up against each other and the match recorded as a half. There's one catch: the captains must put the names of their players in the envelopes prior to start of play, so no matter how bad your boy may be playing, he can't "suddenly" be injured and added to the envelope. This strange situation has only occurred three times since 1979, most recently in 1993 at Belfry.

• The United States and Europe alternate hosting the Ryder Cup.

• Each member of a two-man team plays his own ball, so four balls are in play on every hole. Each team counts the lowest of its two scores on each hole, and the team whose player has the lowest score wins the hole. If the low scores are tied, the hole is halved.

• On top of the Ryder Cup trophy there is a golfer. This is no generic golfing figure. British professional golfer Abe Mitchell adorns the trophy and happened to be the friend and golf instructor of Samuel Ryder. Mitchell competed in three Ryder Cup competitions.

• Captain's choice: The "Captain's Pick" system was introduced in 1979, and since then, United States picks have won 46 percent, while European picks have won 52 percent of their matches.

THE OPEN

It is only fitting to dedicate a cocktail to the birthplace of golf, Scotland. The Open, or the Open Championship, as it's often termed, is the oldest tournament in golf and arguably the most prestigious. I love tuning in to watch the Open simply for the fact of how different it is compared to other golf tournaments. When you first turn to the channel carrying the Open, you're likely to see brutal winds and rain—conditions ill-suited for golf—but the players play on, walking the link-style course that at first glance looks like green chaos. Often the courses have no definitive fairways but plenty of treacherous bunkers and hip-high grass capable of devouring golf balls with only the slightest miscues from the greatest players on earth. Because the tournament rotates among sites in the UK, I wanted to create a drink using a peaty Scotch—Laphroaig, a favorite of mine—along with sage simple syrup and egg white to create an earthy, rich texture.

Clarety

> 1 ¾ oz. bourbon
> ¼ oz. Laphroaig scotch
> ¾ oz. sage simple syrup*
> ½ oz. lemon juice
> Egg white
> Sage leaves

Sage simple syrup Combine 1 cup water with 1 cup sugar in a saucepan over medium heat, and stir until sugar has fully dissolved. Add one pack of sage leaves (about 10 to 15) to the syrup and simmer for ten to fifteen minutes. Remove from heat and let cool prior to using.

<u>Here's How</u> Add egg white to shaker and dry shake (no ice) for ten seconds. Add all remaining ingredients and shake with ice. Strain into rocks glass with one large, round ice cube. Garnish with lemon twist.

How 'Bout That!

- The first Open Championship was played on October 17, 1860, at Prestwick Golf Club in Scotland. A field of eight professionals played three rounds of Prestwick's twelve-hole course in one day.
- Call it what you will: the British Open is officially called the Open Championship, or the Open. It's called the Open because it was the first Open Championship that was, in theory, open to amateur golfers and professionals. Americans continue to call it the British Open to differentiate the tournament from the US Open.
- The tournament is organized by the Royal and Ancient Golf Club of St. Andrews (R&A), the governing body of golf outside of the United States and Mexico.
- Play on, Player: Gary Player has the most appearances in the British Open at a whopping forty-six.
- A victory toast: If you're a fan of golf, you're familiar with the Claret Jug, the trophy that is actually a copy of a real claret jug, which is given to the winner of the British Open. It's been awarded every year since 1872. Claret is a dry red wine that was made in France during nineteenth-century gatherings and served in silver jugs, which is what the trophy was modeled after. Although the championship trophy is officially named the Championship Cup, it's widely referred to as the Claret Jug.
- For the first thirty years of the Open Championship, the tournament was only played in Scotland, until 1894, when the British Open ventured to England. The British

Open is only played on one of nine links courses that are set in either England or Scotland.

- Three and done: Under the original rules of competition, if a player won three times in a row, he was entitled to keep the prize. This basically meant that there was nothing to play for in 1871, so no Open was held that year.

- In 1995, the Open became part of the PGA Tour's official schedule. John Daly won that year after a playoff with Italy's Costantino Rocca, beginning another period of American supremacy at the Open in which ten of the next thirteen winners hailed from the United States.

- Tee-time matters: The Open Championship has always been played on links courses, which are usually treeless courses along the coast that have retained their uneven terrain. Unlike the play of other majors—which are typically contested in sunny locales in the United States—the result of the Open is often dictated by the weather. On a links course, morning and afternoon tee times can produce vastly different playing conditions, depending on the breeze that comes in off the sea.

PGA CHAMPIONSHIP

It feels as though the PGA Championship—one of the four majors in golf—gets overshadowed by more well-known majors, such as the Masters, the Open, and the US Open. The tournament has hosted its share of big-name winners, but no one has been a winner more times than the Golden Bear himself, Jack Nicklaus, who has five titles. An Australian sportswriter coined the "Golden Bear" nickname for Nicklaus at the 1967 US Open based on his burly physique and blond hair. It didn't hurt that Nicklaus attended Upper Arlington High School in Columbus, Ohio, a school whose mascot is the Golden Bears. In creating the Bear of Burden, I wanted to make a cocktail in honor of the

Golden Bear and his record eighteen majors, a burden felt by all golfers following in his tracks, especially Tiger Woods, who is only three majors behind. The addition of goat milk seemed fitting, given Nicklaus's status as arguably the GOAT (greatest of all time) of golf.

Bear of Burden

1 ½ oz. brandy
½ oz. crème de cacao
2 oz. goat milk
½ oz. honey syrup*
¼ oz. fresh lemon juice

*Honey syrup Combine equal parts honey and warm water. Wisk until honey is fully incorporated with water.

<u>Here's How</u> In a mixing glass with ice, shake all ingredients. Strain into a rocks glass over one large, round ice cube. Garnish with lemon twist.

How 'Bout That!

- The first PGA Championship was held at the Siwanoy Country Club in Bronxville, New York.
- In 1917–1918 and 1943, the PGA Championship was suspended for two years due to World Wars I and II.
- On April 10, 1916, the Professional Golfers Association (PGA) of America was formed.
- Oldie, but goodie: Julius Boros was the oldest player to win the PGA Championship at forty-eight years, four months, and eighteen days in 1968.
- The purse for the first PGA Championship back in 1916 was $2,580, with $500 going to the winner. The winner received $100,000 for the first time in 1983 and $1 million for the first time in 2003.

- Before changing to stroke play in 1958, the PGA Championship was the only major to use match play as its format.

- Chasing the Bear: In the modern era, Jack Nicklaus holds the most PGA Championship titles with five, followed by Tiger Woods with four.

- Not so fast, young guns: The only way an amateur can participate in the tournament is if they've won any of the four major championships. Winners of the PGA Championship are given a lifelong invitation to the event, while the previous five winners of the US Open, Masters, and British Open are invited annually.

- Better be in shape at the Hollow: The length of four rounds at Quail Hollow is 30,400 yards, equivalent to 17.3 miles, or 66 percent of a marathon.

- Step right up: Vacancies at the PGA Championship are filled by the first available player from the list of alternates (players below seventieth place in the PGA Championship points list from the previous year's World Golf Championships—the Bridgestone Invitational through the current year's RBC Canadian Open).

- The Big Prize: The PGA Championship trophy, one of the largest in golf, is named after department store magnate Rodman Wanamaker, a keen golfer and man partly responsible for founding the PGA. The winner of the tournament gets to hold on to a replica of the Wanamaker trophy for one year. The original trophy briefly went missing after golfing legend Walter Hagen claimed he "lost" it in 1928. It was coincidentally found two years later in the basement of the manufacturer of Hagen's golf club line. Very interesting. . . . The Wanamaker Trophy weighs twenty-seven pounds, though it probably feels as light as a feather to whoever is fortunate to hoist it at the end of the tournament.

- In 2015, Jason Day became the first player to finish twenty under par in a major at the PGA Championship.

4
Hockey

THE STANLEY CUP

There is no greater trophy in sports than the Stanley Cup. Period. Hockey has always been a part of my life, thanks to my father, Pierre, who grew up playing hockey in Montreal and idolizing the Montreal Canadiens. Canada may have only seven franchises in the NHL, but the sport means far more to native Canadians than it does to us down here in the United States. We certainly appreciate the game, but the game is not, as a whole, part of our identity as Americans. For Americans, baseball or football would fill this cultural spot. My family attended a maple sugar festival in Quebec, and if you've ever tasted pure maple syrup compared to the artificial syrup lining grocery store shelves, you know what a superior product real maple syrup is. My goal was to create a drink using Canadian staples—whisky and maple syrup—that's perfect for sipping while watching grown men battle for hockey immortality and the right to have their names etched on the Stanley Cup.

Lord Stanley Sour

1 ½ oz. Pendleton Blended Canadian Whisky
½ oz. Jack Daniels Honey
¾ oz. Canadian maple syrup
1 oz. lemon juice
Egg white
Bordeaux maraschino cherry (garnish)
Lemon twist (garnish)

<u>Here's How</u> In a mixing glass, add all ingredients and dry shake (no ice) for ten seconds. Add ice and remaining ingredients to the shaker and shake for eight to twelve seconds more. Strain into a rocks glass over one large cube and garnish with Bordeaux maraschino cherry and lemon twist.

How 'Bout That!

• Step aside, billionaires: After all the blood, sweat, and tears of the playoffs, the Stanley Cup goes to the players first before the owners. Look closely and you'll even see the coaches step aside to let the players raise the Cup first.

• Lord Stanley of Preston was governor-general of Canada in 1892 and actually bought the Cup on a trip to London. It was the 1889 Winter Carnival in Montreal where he and his family fell in love with hockey. He donated the Cup to the top amateur hockey team in Canada. Look closely and you'll

see that the first names engraved on the Cup belong to the players in the 1893 Montreal Amateur Athletic Association.

• Hab-itual Champions: the Montreal Canadiens (Habs) hold the record for most Stanley Cup victories, with twenty-four in the books.

• The Cup belongs to each winning player for a day, and the NHL permits the champions to spend one hundred off-season days with the Cup.

• No pressure or anything: Two babies have been baptized in the Cup. I can just hear the dad now when his son—who, again, was baptized in the Stanley Cup—refuses to play the game.

"Will you at least try? At least try and skate or hold this stick and hit the puck! You were baptized in the Cup, for God's sake."

"I never asked for any of this!"

• Oldie, but goodie: Unlike other sports, a new Stanley Cup trophy is not made every year. When players hoist the Cup, they're lifting the same Cup they dreamed of winning as children. All players, coaches, and management names are etched on the trophy and part of hockey history forever.

• The Cup is always changing as new names are added every year. Obviously with all the names, the Cup would be too long to lift, so rings must be removed. The names of players between 1928–1929 and 1953–1954 are at the Hockey Hall of Fame.

• Boozin' Bears: the Boston Bruins managed to rack up a $156,679.74 bar tab during their Stanley Cup celebration at MGM Grand at Foxwoods Resort Casino. One hundred thousand dollars of that bill was on one bottle of champagne.

• Messier and the clubs: Mark Messier of the 1986–1987 Stanley Cup–winning Edmonton Oilers took the Cup to a strip club and set the trophy on the main stage, where a dancer at the club incorporated the Cup into her routine. Not one apparently to shy from the strip clubs, Messier, after winning another Cup in 1994 with the Rangers, took the Cup to the Scores gentlemen's club in Manhattan.

• Fishing with the greats: Mario Lemieux of the Pittsburg Penguins held a team party at his house, where the Cup went for a dip in Mario's pool. Phil Bourque, the creative genius behind the trophy toss, wanted to see if the Cup would float. It did not, which Patrick Roy proved again two years later when the Stanley Cup found its way to the bottom of his pool.

• Lord of War: To boost morale for American and Canadian troops serving in the Middle East, Lord Stanley's Cup was flown into an active war zone at Camp Nathan Smith in Kandahar, Afghanistan, for a meet and greet of sorts.

NHL WINTER CLASSIC

The NHL Winter Classic is hockey the way it's meant to be played: outside, in the cold, with snow falling and the fans bundled up in scarfs and sweaters. Gordie Howe, Mr. Hockey himself, would be proud of the NHL and its decision to make the Winter Classic happen every January. My father grew up in Montreal, Canada, and played hockey every week on the nearby frozen ponds. Like so many other young Montreal boys, he dreamed of playing for the Montreal Canadiens and taking his skills from the frozen ponds to a packed arena, the Forum, as it stood for so many years in downtown Montreal. The Winter Classic is so fun to watch because it combines the outdoor aspect with the raucous fans who fill whatever MLB ballpark the NHL decides to use as its venue. And you better believe there's plenty of hot chocolate being sipped by those fans in the stands. Smoke on the Ice is homemade hot chocolate with caramel and orange zest, combined with smoky mezcal to truly warm you up as you watch the NHL's best battle it out in hockey's truest form.

Smoke on the Ice

(2 servings)
1 ½ oz. mezcal
2 cups whole milk
2 oz. dark chocolate wafers (for melting)
2 oz. salted caramel chips
Orange zest (from one orange)
Whipped cream*
2 tbsp. sugar
1 cup chilled heavy whipping cream
1 tsp. vanilla extract

*Whipped cream Prior to making whipped cream, place your mixing bowl and whisk in the freezer to chill for about fifteen minutes. Add sugar and vanilla extract along with heavy whipping cream to the bowl. Whisk together until stiff peaks form. Cover and cool in refrigerator until ready to use.

<u>Here's How</u> Chop chocolate into small pieces, place in microwave-safe bowl with salted caramel chips, and heat until melted

(start with twenty seconds). In a saucepan, heat milk over medium-high heat until milk begins to bubble along the edges, making sure the milk does not come to a boil (which would cause the hot chocolate to separate). Remove milk from heat once it has begun bubbling and whisk in melted chocolate, caramel and orange zest. Continually stir with a whisk until chocolate is fully incorporated. Pour in glass and add mezcal (or brandy if you're not onboard with the smokiness of mezcal). Top with whipped cream and garnish with orange wedge.

How 'Bout That!

- The first Winter Classic almost took place in 2004. Jon Miller, president of programming for NBC and NBCSN, pitched the idea of playing a game at Yankee Stadium between the Boston Bruins and New York Rangers. The idea came only a few months after the Red Sox rallied to beat the Yankees in the American League Championship Series. The network had space to fill, as college football was no longer in its lineup. There was resistance from the league, so it didn't come to fruition until 2008. The Pittsburgh Penguins and Buffalo Sabres played in the inaugural NHL Winter Classic in 2008 when they faced off on a snowy New Year's Day at Ralph Wilson Stadium in Buffalo, New York. Only one Winter Classic was not played on New Year's Day.

- The 2012 Winter Classic featuring the Flyers and Rangers was played on January 2 because January 1 was a Sunday and NBC was worried about its primetime NFL game. If a weather delay had pushed the afternoon start to a night start, NBC would have had a scheduling conflict. And the pigskins win again.

- Pittsburgh Penguins captain Sidney Crosby led his team to victory over the Sabres with a shootout goal in the inaugural Winter Classic in 2008.

- There was no Winter Classic in 2013 due to the lockout.
- According to *Forbes*, the average cost of a ticket for the Winter Classic is about $500, the highest rate in five years. As of December 3, the cheapest ticket on StubHub for the 2015 Winter Classic was $215, with club seats going for as much as $2,800.

- Fill 'er up! Three thousand gallons of coolant is pumped from a truck to the rink to maintain a certain temperature. Workers will then spray twenty thousand gallons of water to get the ice to a thickness of two inches, perfect for outdoor hockey. That water will be added as slowly as possible while workers pass the spray wand over the surface hundreds of times. Rather than just flooding the rink with a hose, workers build the ice with about 200 to 220 fine layers over about eight days. Ultimately, the ice will reach a depth of about two inches, a bit thicker than an indoor rink. Workers will then whiten the ice using 350 gallons of water-soluble paint before the lines and logos are painted. Finally, more ice will be added on top.

- The NHL's one-of-a-kind three-hundred-ton mobile refrigeration unit is in charge of making sure the ice is fit for the Winter Classic.

5
Baseball

The Super Bowl may have surpassed the World Series in terms of popularity in the United States, but the World Series remains a staple of American culture. There is no better time in baseball than October, when playoff series are in full swing as teams battle for the right to compete in the World Series. I grew up in Roanoke, Virginia, and we have a minor league team that plays about fifteen minutes from my childhood house. Watching baseball was great, but what really sticks in my mind is the food and drink at the ballpark. A box of Cracker Jack and a Coke—is there anything better in life? Maybe throw in a hot dog or two to really send life over the top! Baseball lore is full of conspiracy theories and curses, none quite as fascinating, or unbelievable, as the curse cast on the Chicago Cubs by a tavern owner in Chicago, who only wanted to watch his Cubs in the World Series . . . with his goat by his side.

Billy Goat Blue

> 2 oz. brandy
> ½ oz. blueberry simple syrup*
> ¼ oz. fresh lemon juice
> 1 oz. goat milk
> Dash of vanilla extract
> Cracker Jack (for cocktail rim)

*Blueberry simple syrup Combine 1 cup of water and 1 cup of granulated sugar in a saucepan over medium heat and stir until all sugar has dissolved. Add 1 cup of fresh blueberries and continue to simmer until blueberries are soft enough to mash. Mash and strain through a fine-mesh sieve or colander. Let cool before using.

<u>Here's How</u> Finely grind Cracker Jack in coffee grinder. Using lemon wedge, moisten half of the outside of the rim of the coupe glass and rim the glass with Cracker Jack. Combine all ingredients in a shaker. Add ice and shake, then strain drink into coupe glass.

How 'Bout That!

- Sure, it may be called the World Series, but only one team from outside the United States has ever won; this honor belongs to Jumpin' Joe Carter and the Toronto Blue Jays, who took the crown in 1992 and 1993.

- Yanks' domination: Of the 112 World Series to date, the Yankees have made it to the World Series on 40 occasions and won 27 times.

- One-time perfection: Don Larsen of the New York Yankees is the only player ever to throw a perfect game, a no-hitter, in MLB postseason history. He accomplished the feat in Game 5 of the 1956 World Series versus a stacked roster for the Brooklyn Dodgers, including Jackie Robinson and Roy Campanella, both hall-of-famers. The Dodgers were defending champions who had defeated the Yankees in the World Series the year prior.

- It wasn't easy getting the World Series to happen. Prior to the World Series, the American Association Champions (a rival organization that folded in 1891) competed versus the National League Champions in an exhibition series. The games were disorganized, hapless events where the series might go on for three games or fifteen, which may have something to do with the teams themselves organizing the United States or World Championship Series. The contempt between the American Association and National League grew as both leagues battled to establish supremacy in the baseball marketplace. Finally, the two sides would get their chance at dominating the other in the first official World Series in 1903, which pitted the Pittsburgh Pirates of the National League versus the Boston Americans. The Americans prevailed.

- It's that damn goat! Billy Sianis, the owner of the Billy Goat Tavern in Chicago, decided to bring his pet goat into Game 4 of the 1945 World Series, which didn't sit well with fans around him. He was forced to leave, as the goat was apparently bothering fans. There's nothing more dehumanizing than asking a man and his goat to leave a baseball game. Sianis was furious. He declared and predicted, and essentially cursed, the Cubs to go World Series–less from that point on, 1945–2016, when the Cubbies finally broke the curse.

- Red Sox fans have a bone to pick with Harry Frazee, the Red Sox owner and theater financier who decided to sell Babe Ruth to the Yankees for $100,000 in cash and a $300,000 loan. Many believed he made the sale to finance the play *No, No, Nanette*. The Bambino made the Sox pay and single-handedly out-homered their entire team in ten of the next twelve seasons. But, hey, who can forget *No, No, Nanette*? Everyone, that's who.

- Many attempts were made to reverse the curse of the Babe. In 1999, the Red Sox decided to bring in Babe Ruth's daughter, Julia Ruth Stevens, to throw out the first pitch in an American League Championship game (as the Babe likely rolled in his grave).

- In order to break the curse, a Tibetan Buddhist monk advised a Red Sox fan to place a Sox cap at the summit of Mount Everest and burn a Yankees cap at Everest Base Camp.

- In July 2004, a foul ball hit by Manny Ramirez flew into the stands, hitting a boy in the face and knocking out two of his teeth. It just so happened that the boy lived in the Sudbury farmhouse that was once owned by Babe Ruth. Fans claimed that event had broken the curse, as the Sox went on to win the World Series that year.

• Traditionally, winners of the World Series receive championship rings. However, this wasn't always the case. In the early part of the twentieth century, players won medallions, pins, or pocket watches as rewards for their athletic achievement. In 1932, rings became the official award. Poor Frank Crosetti of the Yankees won so many rings with the Yankees—seven as a player, ten as a coach—that he ran out of fingers to adorn them with. So, instead of rings, Frank was awarded engraved shotguns, and the fowl population in New York State greatly diminished, I'm assuming.

MLB ALL-STAR GAME

As far as sports all-star games go, Major League Baseball provides a very good one, most likely because the star players don't alter their game in order to play. In the NFL Pro Bowl, players, rightfully so, are concerned with their careers and getting injured. The same goes for the NHL, where its all-star game feels more like a pickup game that, yes, is loaded with skill and talent, but lacks the emotion and physicality of the regular season and playoffs. Baseball is different. The best pitchers pitch their best, and the best batters swat it all around the ballpark. And nothing beats the Home Run Derby, a favorite event for fans to watch their favorite sluggers. What we often forget about with baseball is just how popular it is around the globe in places like the Dominican Republic, Cuba, and, most surprisingly to me, South Korea, Taiwan, and the Philippines. The South Pacific incorporates ingredients found in the Pacific region of the world, including sake, ginger, and lemongrass, and speaks to just how popular the game of baseball is across the globe.

The South Pacific

2 oz. vodka
¾ oz. medium-dry sake
¾ oz. cherry brandy
1 oz. Asian pear puree
¼ oz. lemon juice
3 slices of ginger
Bordeaux maraschino cherries (garnish)
Lemon twist (garnish)

<u>Here's How</u> Add pear puree, lemon juice, and ginger to a mixing glass and gently muddle. Add ice, vodka, sake, and cherry brandy. Shake well and strain through a double strainer into coupe glass and garnish with cherries and lemon twist on a cocktail spear.

How 'Bout That!

• From 1959 to 1962, there were two All-Star Games each season, which were played back-to-back, giving top players of the day four more games to add to their All-Star statistics.

• Although baseball has been around since before 1900, it wasn't until 1933 that the two leagues deliberately met in the middle of the season to play each other. Why the sudden need to test each league's strength? There was a World's Fair in Chicago in 1933, and a sports editor proposed the idea to have a game between the best players from each league. The game was held in Comiskey Park, home of the Chicago White Sox.

• Another notch on the Babe's belt: Babe Ruth hit the first All-Star home run, a two-run shot to right field off the Cardinals' Bill Hallahan in 1933. The American League won the game 4–2.

- A grand feat for only one: There has been only one grand slam in all eighty-six All-Star Games. The shot was delivered by Fred Lynn of the California Angels in the 1983 game. The fact that the best hitters get nine innings to swing away and have only accomplished this feat once . . . that deserves a tip of the cap for all the aces on the mound.

- The Home Run Derby, played the day before the All-Star Game, began in 1985. Dave Winfield won the first contest, which was held in the Metrodome in Minneapolis.

- Are we there yet? The All-Star Game is the unofficial halfway point of the season, which is why it's also known as the Midsummer Classic.

- The American League—the younger of the two leagues—is sometimes referred to as the "Junior" League. However, over the last two decades, the National League has won only three times, and those were in succession from 2010 to 2012.

- Reds spoiled it for everyone: In 1957, Cincinnati fans stuffed the ballot box and elected Reds to every position except Stan Musial at first base. Commissioner Ford Frick took charge and replaced Gus Bell and Wally Post with Hank Aaron and Willie Mays, then took the voting away from fans. You can't argue with those two solid substitutions.

- Speaking of Hank: Hank Aaron of the Braves played in more All-Star Games, twenty-five, than any other player. Willie Mays and Stan Musial played in twenty-four All-Star Games each.

- Good news for everyone who hates home runs! Don Drysdale holds the all-time record for career All-Star Game strikeouts with nineteen, and fifteen pitchers have recorded at least five strikeouts in a single ASG, with Pedro Martinez in 1999, being the last.

One refreshing aspect of the College World Series is the sense of parity in terms of champions. Unlike college football, which is typically dominated by a handful of schools, past winners of the CWS include Vanderbilt, Oregon State, Florida, Coastal Carolina, UCLA, and Arizona—just to name a few. If there is a team that has enjoyed a bit of dominance at the World Series, it would have to be the University of Southern California, a school that boasts a .740 winning percentage at the annual event in Omaha, Nebraska. But the other schools are catching up given that USC has not won a College World Series title since 1998. My goal was to create a bright summer drink that incorporates strawberries since the College World Series takes place as the summer is just getting underway. The cocktail is red, as the perennial host of the event is Omaha, in Nebraska, a state that certainly bleeds red (Go Huskers!).

It's Always Sunny in Omaha

1 ½ oz. gin
½ oz. elderflower liqueur
¾ oz. simple syrup
¾ lemon juice
4 ripe strawberries
2 mint sprigs
2 dashes balsamic vinegar

<u>Here's How</u> In a mixing glass, muddle 2 strawberries and 1 mint sprig. Add remaining ingredients and shake well. Strain into a Collins glass and garnish with remaining mint and strawberries.

How 'Bout That!

- The inaugural College World Series was held in 1947 and was an eight-team tournament held in Kalamazoo, Michigan. University of California swept Yale to win the first CWS.

• Not always Home, Sweet Home: Before determining Omaha as the permanent home for the College World Series, the tournament was held in two other locations: Kalamazoo, Michigan, and Wichita, Kansas, which hosted from 1947–1949, until Omaha was declared home in 1950.

• Bush league: Before becoming commander in chief, George H. W. Bush spent his days on the diamond. Bush played first base and captained the 1948 Yale baseball team that lost in the championship round to, you guessed it, Southern California. George W. Bush was the first president to attend the College World Series, and in 2001, he threw out the first pitch.

• As of 2012, more than eight million fans have attended the College World Series in Omaha.

• Leading up to the College World Series is the NCAA Division I Baseball Championship tournament in May, which features sixty-four college baseball teams battling it out in a series of elimination games. Winners of the regionals are given spots in the Super Regional games located throughout the country. Two teams go head-to-head at each location for a best-of-three game series. Super Regional action finishes around midmonth as teams left standing clinch their World Series spots.

• Not finished yet! Barry Bonds is one of the most notable college players to make it in the pros. Others to emerge from the College World Series include Will Clark, Roger Clemens, J. D. Drew, and Robin Ventura, among many others.

• ESPN televised selected College World Series games for the first time in 1980. The broadcast was a ratings hit.

• The all-time attendance record at the College World Series is 336,072, set in 2009.

• Prime Time in the prime of his time: Deion Sanders, one of the greatest athletes in Florida State history, not only led his Seminoles football team to the Sugar Bowl, but he also helped the baseball team make the College World Series. Not a bad tenure in school. Sadly, Sanders's Seminoles have made the tournament more times than any other school (twenty-one) without winning a championship.

• Southern California has won the College World Series more than any other team in the nation. The Trojans have 12 championships, which is double its next closest competition: LSU and Texas.

• Twelfth time's a charm! After twelve appearances at the College World Series, the Florida Gators finally claimed victory in 2017.

6
Tennis

WIMBLEDON

Tradition reigns supreme at the All England Club in Wimbledon, London. Traditions include having competitors dress almost entirely in white, playing on grass courts, eating strawberries and cream, and sipping on a Pimm's Cup, which is *the* drink of the Wimbledon tournament held in July. In keeping with tradition, I created a cocktail to make at home while watching the tournament that incorporates these components, while adding other elements, such as Bombay gin, which is just so very British that it had to be a part of the cocktail. Midori melon liqueur adds a nice, sweet touch to the cocktail while also lending its unique color as an homage to the grass courts at Wimbledon.

Lawn Service

1 oz. Bombay gin
½ oz. Pimm's Liqueur
½ oz. St. Germain Elderflower Liqueur
1 ½ oz. Midori
½ oz. lemon juice
Splash of lemon-lime soda
Strawberry (garnish)
Lemon (garnish)

<u>Here's How</u> Add all ingredients, except lemon-lime soda, to a mixing glass with ice. Shake and strain in Collins glass. Garnish with strawberry and lemon.

How 'Bout That!

- Wimbledon is the oldest tennis tournament in the world. On June 9, 1877, the first Wimbledon Championship took place on Worple Road.

- The landlord of an oyster bar, James Pimm, invented Pimm's No. 1, a gin-based herbal-citrus liqueur, in 1840 and marketed it as a health tonic and digestive aid. About 320,000 glasses of Pimm's is sold annually at the tournament along with 140,000 portions of English strawberries.

- Wimbledon was originally open to amateurs, but the word "amateur" meant something else entirely years ago. "Amateur" did not signify a lesser competitor, but actually stood for a gentleman. "Professional" held the connotation of laborer and, thus, not suited for the Wimbledon Championship. Professional athletes began playing at the tournament in 1968.

- Martina Navratilova won more Wimbledon singles crowns (9) than any person in history, Open Era or pre–Open Era, men or women. Navratilova won her first Wimbledon singles title as a twenty-one-year-old Czech and her last one as a thirty-three-year-old American. She made a groundbreaking announcement in 1981 in which she came out as lesbian, which became a factor in social change.

- Cold fuzz: Fifty-four thousand tennis balls are used over the course of the Championship and are refrigerated at sixty-eight degrees to keep them looking spotless.

- The tradition of tennis whites began more than 125 years ago in the 1800s when white clothing was worn to avoid perspiration stains. It was an abomination, an unthinkable blasphemy, that a woman would be seen to perspire, even during athletic competition. Men were not immune to the "whiteness of it all," and gentlemen with dark arm hair were said to have been asked to bleach their arm hair.

• Hawk-eye technology: Every morning during the tournament, a Harris's hawk named Rufus is released over the grounds at the All England Club to scare away the pigeons that are looking for leftovers or planning to defecate on the courts below—the one form of white club organizers refuse to accept.

• Catered to the masses: The Wimbledon Championship is the largest catering operation in Europe, with more than 3,000 staff members.

US OPEN

It's New York City. It's September. It's competition under the lights—it's the US Open of tennis. The buzz surrounding the US Open and exhilaration of playing under the bright lights of New York is palpable, and my goal was to match that buzz with a bright, effervescent buzz of your own. The tournament is the fourth major tournament of the year and arguably the most exciting. When I think of excitement and anticipation, I'm drawn toward Champagne and a drink that physically looks "alive" with the bubbles rushing toward the rim of the glass. The Anjou pear adds a nice fall touch to the cocktail, as the men's and women's finals are held in September, when there's a light chill in the air and in your glass.

Under the Lights

1 oz. pear-infused vodka
½ oz. fresh lemon juice
½ oz. simple syrup
Champagne (to top)
Anjou pear (quarter for muddling, slice for garnish)

<u>Here's How</u> In a mixing glass, muddle the pear, then add the vodka, lemon juice, and simple syrup. Shake with ice and strain into a champagne flute. Top with Champagne and garnish with pear slice.

How 'Bout That!

- All's fair in love and hard courts. Prize money at the US Open is awarded equally between men and women, which started in 1973 thanks to Billie Jean King, who threatened to boycott after receiving $10,000 for her win in 1972, which was 40 percent less than the men's winner, who received $25,000. It took other majors a while longer to catch on and award prize money equally, which happened in 2001.
- Easy money, kind of: If a player makes the tournament and never wins a match, they are still guaranteed $54,000.

Win the first round, but lose in the second, a player will still walk away with $93,000. Not bad for a loser.

- The US Open trophy is designed by Tiffany & Co.
- Grass past: The US Open wasn't always played on hard courts. Until 1974, the tournament was played on grass courts, then clay for three years. Finally, in 1978, the US Open moved to its current home with hard courts named after Billie Jean King. Jimmy Connors is the only player who has won the tournament on all three surfaces.
- Arthur Ashe won the tournament as an amateur. Still a lieutenant in the US Army, Ashe had yet to give up his amateur status when he defeated Tom Okker and was paid as an amateur, making only $280 total, or $20 per day for the fourteen days of competition. Ashe became the first, and only, African American male tennis player to win the US Open and Wimbledon and the first African American man to be ranked as the number one tennis player in the world.
- Steffi Graf, one of the greatest female tennis players of all time, won the US Open five times. She reached thirteen consecutive Grand Slam finals and is the only player in history to have achieved the "Golden Slam," a term made up especially for the feat she achieved. That feat was winning a gold at the Olympics and all four Grand Slams in the same year.
- The US Open boasts the largest tennis-specific stadium in the world. Named in honor of Arthur Ashe, the stadium holds 23,771 fans. Who cares if you have to tend to your bleeding nose the entire event and can hardly make out the players on the court—and forget about seeing the ball—you're still there, you made it!
- Bad shot: During a match between John McEnroe and Eddie Dibbs in 1977, a gunshot rang out that briefly stopped play. It was later found that a fan had been shot in the leg by a stray bullet from outside the grounds.

The Australian Open is the first of the four tennis Grand Slams and, in my opinion, an underrated event in the United States. The Grand Slam is in fact the largest annual sporting event in the Southern Hemisphere. It took a while for the tournament to catch on with players from outside of Australia and New Zealand—many competitors decided to skip the trip on account of the long travel time and remoteness of the continent. But now all the greatest tennis players on earth partake in the competition, which is oftentimes grueling on account of the summer temperatures in Melbourne. My goal with Donkey Down Under was to create a light, refreshing cocktail using one of Australia's great exports: Bundaberg Ginger Beer. The cucumber and lavender gin enhance the cocktail's appeal, especially on those brutally hot days. Of course, if you're watching in the Northern Hemisphere, you might be a little chilly—nothing a little ginger beer can't remedy.

Donkey Down Under

1 ½ oz. lavender gin
½ oz. lime juice
Bundaberg Ginger Beer
3 slices fresh cucumber (muddled, garnish)

<u>Here's How</u> In a mixing glass, muddle two slices of cucumber. Add gin and lime juice. Shake well with ice and strain into copper mug. Top with ginger beer and garnish with cucumber.

How 'Bout That!

• When the Australian Open first began in 1905, the game was played on a grass turf, and the trend continued until 1987. From 1988 onward, the tournament made its first change by introducing hard courts to replace the grass.

- Bloody hell, it's a hot time of year to be playing tennis! The Australian Open is held in January every year—summer in Australia. The daytime temperature can rise up to forty-five degrees Celsius, which is well above one hundred degrees Fahrenheit. Many players have to be put on intravenous drips in order to cope with the blistering weather conditions in Melbourne. The Australian Open makes use of EHP, or Extreme Heat Policy, under which umpires can suspend any given tennis match when the temperature soars. Introduced in 1998, it calls for play to be stopped on all courts once the temperature reaches 104 degrees Fahrenheit.

- In order to cope up with the heat, many retractable roofs have been constructed and provide some relief to players and fans.

- The inaugural Australian Open was held on a cricket ground. The tournament was held at the Warehouseman's Cricket Ground at Melbourne, which is now called the Albert Reserve Tennis Centre.

- American Chris Evert won the Australian Open two times and created a huge rivalry with fellow great Martina Navratilova. They met thirteen times in finals, on every type of surface, with Evert only managing to win three of those showdowns. However, Evert, who held the title of world number one for seven years, has the greatest ever win-loss record in singles matches (.900), male or female.

- Each year, the tournament uses around 40,000 tennis balls. To handle them, more than 300 ball boys and girls volunteer every year.

- The Australian Open is the only tennis tournament to have been played in two different countries: Australia and New Zealand. In the early days, the tournament was known as the Australasian Open. In 1972, Melbourne was selected as the tournament's official venue, and the major has been held there every year since.

- In 2012, the final between Rafael Nadal and Novak Djokovic lasted for five hours and fifty-three minutes, becoming the longest final in Grand Slam history. The Serbian came out as the winner, by 5–7, 6–4, 6–2, 6–7 (5–7), 7–5.
- Mats Wilander is the only player to have won the tournament on both hard and grass courts.
- Johnny B Bad: When it comes to on-court outbursts, no one compares with John McEnroe. In 1990, the American tennis legend became the first player to be disqualified from the Australian Open after telling the umpire to do something less than civil with his mother.
- Thanks, but no thanks: Many of the top players during the 1970s and 1980s opted not to play the tournament, citing the remoteness of the country, inconvenient dates, and low prize money as primary reasons for skipping the tournament down under.

French Open

There's no mistaking the French Open for other tennis tournaments; the red clay courts give it away. I was fortunate to have the opportunity to play tennis on a clay court and gained an immediate respect for the surface and the competitors who play elite tennis on clay at Roland-Garros every year. The tournament is regarded as the most strenuous and physically demanding of the all the tennis tournaments, thanks in large part to the slow-playing surface and the seven rounds needed to secure a championship. Roland, Red Roland was created to honor and resemble the clay courts at Roland-Garros. The cocktail is topped with champagne, an obvious nod to Paris, the French, and their supremacy when it comes to the sparkling wine.

Roland, Red Roland

¾ oz. sloe gin
¾ oz. Campari
¾ oz. dry vermouth
2 dashes orange bitters
Champagne
Orange spiral (garnish)

<u>Here's How</u> Combine all ingredients in a mixing glass and stir for twenty to thirty seconds. Strain using julep strainer into a coupe glass. Top with champagne. Garnish with orange spiral.

How 'Bout That!

• The term "French Open" is more recognized across the globe, but the French actually call the Grand Slam "Roland-Garros." Roland Garros was a French aviator who was the first pilot to fly over the Mediterranean Sea. If that wasn't enough, he also fought in the World War I. Garros gained notoriety another way by developing a means of allowing a machine gun to be fired forward through a plane's propeller arc.

• And now for the timeline:

• 1940–1945: The tournament is canceled due to World War II.

• 1989: Michael Chang becomes the youngest man ever to win the singles title at seventeen years and three months of age.

• 2006: The French Open awards equal prize money to the men's and women's singles champions, although disparity remains in all other rounds.

• 2020: Nadal wins his 13th French Open title and 20th overall Grand Slam singles title.

• Solo Musketeer: The prize for winning the men's singles event is called the Musketeers' Cup. Who are these musketeers? The musketeers are legendary French tennis stars René Lacoste, Henri Cochet, Jacques Brugnon, and Jean Borotra. The four won ten singles titles between 1922 and 1932. Nothing, however, trumped their Davis Cup win in 1927—as a reward for their efforts, a stadium was erected dedicated to the defense of their title. The arena would eventually be named after Roland Garros, the aviation pioneer who was killed in combat during the Great War.

• The French Clay-Court Championships was created in 1891, and the tournament was reserved for players who were members of French clubs. The tournament was held at venues alternating between the Parc de Saint-Cloud, the Stade Francais, and the Racing Club de France's Croix-Catelan grounds. The first big change came in 1925 when the competition was opened up to players outside of France. Thus, the French Open was born.

• Not so easy on this clay stuff: Many of the big names of the tennis world have never won at Roland-Garros. Take for instance, legends like Martina Hingis and Venus Williams. On the men's side, tennis greats John McEnroe, Pete Sampras, and Jimmy Connors are all title-less on the clay.

• The use of clay was originally a practical consideration. In Cannes in 1880, the Renshaw brothers used powdered terra-cotta to cover grass courts to keep them from wilting in the heat, and today the concept remains the same—with a few added technological advances of course.

• Not quite as much clay as one might think: Individual layers of stone, gravel, volcanic residue, limestone, and crushed brick make up the clay court. Players who compete on these courts are expected to have better stamina because the games on clay courts not only exhaust the players more quickly, but they also last longer.

7
Soccer

FIFA World Cup

The world is watching, literally. Half of the world's population watched the World Cup in 2018 in Russia—about 3.572 billion people. The United States may not be legitimate contenders to bring home the trophy, but it's sure fun as hell to root them on. Soccer, or "futbol," as the game is more properly referred to around the world, is so popular because of its accessibility. Anybody can play anywhere. First-world and third-world countries alike can produce the most spectacular talents.

My wife and I visited Cuba and found that the Cuban people seem to carry themselves with a unique rhythm for life, a joy of being. Sure, this could stem from the rum that flows across the island. Our trip coincided with the Champions League Final, and we watched the game in the basement of a small hotel just outside Viñales. The hotel basement was full of rabid fans all brandishing the jerseys of their favorite players, and bottles of rum were being passed around at each table as fans gnawed on giant turkey legs. Watching a soccer game in Cuba proved to me just how important this game, this religion, is to people around the world. My goal was to create a bright, optimistic cocktail full of flavor and life. The keyword for this cocktail, for the World Cup as a whole, is passion, and passiflora, or passionflower, which produces the passion fruit, is a great symbol the world's love for futbol.

Passiflora Fizz

1 ½ oz. Breckenridge Spiced Rum
½ oz. passion fruit simple syrup*
½ oz. fresh lime juice
3 sprigs basil (muddling, garnish)
2 orange slices (muddling, garnish)
Club soda

*Passion fruit simple syrup In a saucepan, combine 1 cup sugar with 1 cup water and bring to a simmer over medium-high heat until sugar has dissolved. Cut 4 to 5 passion fruits in half and scoop out the fruit pulp to add to the saucepan. Simmer briefly, about five minutes, then remove from heat and let steep for an hour. Strain contents through a fine-mesh sieve into glass and let cool prior to using.

<u>Here's How</u> In a mixing glass, muddle 2 basil sprigs and 1 orange slice. Add remaining ingredients along with ice. Shake and strain into a rocks glass with one large cube and top with club soda. Garnish with orange slice and basil.

How 'Bout That!

• All World Cups have been won by European or South American sides. Europe has eleven titles, while South American teams have nine.

• Planet Earth is watching: Roughly 46 percent of the world's population, or 3.2 billion people, watched more than one minute of the World Cup in 2010, making the tournament, according to FIFA, the "world's most widely viewed sporting event."

• Relatively generous: FIFA awards the winning team of the World Cup $35 million. The runner-up gets $25 million. Sounds incredible, right? Well, considering FIFA generally makes around $4.6 billion over the course of the tournament, $60 million in prize money doesn't exactly propel FIFA to sainthood.

• Streets of liquid gold: In South Africa during the 2010 World Cup, more than 750,000 liters of beer were sold in stadiums hosting the tournament. For an impressive conversion, that's 3,170,064 beers.

- Founded in 1904, FIFA (International Federation of Association Football) is governed by Swiss Law and is headquartered in Zurich. FIFA is considered the "United Nations of Football" and has 209 members.

- Brazil is the only country to play in every World Cup and holds the record for most titles with five, with Germany and Italy in a close second with four titles each. Brazil has won 25 percent of the World Cups held.

- Ah, come on, Coach, just this once! Many coaches actually ban their players from having sex during the World Cup: Germany, Spain, Mexico, and Chile all forbid fornication. Apparently, managers cite sex as a distraction and waste of the players' energy; the players likely disagree. But some managers are a bit more lenient. Brazil's Luiz Felipe Scolari allows his players to have sex, but he instructs them to abstain from "acrobatic" forms of sex. So, any teams with players doing bicycle kicks on the field are not having acrobatic sex off the pitch. Save it for the match, guys!

- In 2019, USA secured its fourth Women's World Cup title (1991, 1999, 2015, and 2019), now winning twice as many Women's World Cup tournaments as any other nation. The USWNT joined Germany as the only two teams in the history of the Women's World Cup to win back-to-back titles.

- The World Cup trophy went missing for seven days in 1966, when it was stolen just prior to the tournament. The tournament was skipped altogether in 1942 and 1946 due to World War II.

- With only 334,000 residents, Iceland is the smallest country, in terms of population, ever to compete in the World Cup.

It's no secret the South American continent is teeming with young, talented soccer players. How could it not be? Soccer is religion in so many parts of the world, especially our American neighbors to the south: Brazil, Argentina, Uruguay, and Colombia—just to name a few of the powerhouse countries that compete at the elite level in the Copa América, the world's oldest soccer tournament. In honor of South America and Brazil, a country that has been so dominant over the years, I use cachaça as the base spirit for the Southern Pitch. Cachaça, a liquor distilled from sugarcane juice, is considered Brazil's national spirit, with the caipirinha the national cocktail of Brazil.

The Southern Pitch

1 ½ oz. cachaça
½ oz. pear liqueur
1 oz. orange spice tea
¼ oz. simple syrup
Lemon (wedge for muddling, wheel for garnish)
Orange (wedge for muddling, wheel for garnish)

<u>Here's How</u> In a mixing glass, muddle the lemon and orange wedges. Add remaining ingredients and shake well. Strain over one large ice cube in a rocks glass and garnish with lemon and orange wheels in the drink.

How 'Bout That!

- The Copa América is the oldest football tournament in the world and is played on the South American continent. Yes, the World Cup was first played in 1930 and the European Championship was founded in 1960, but the Copa América started in 1916, making it the world's oldest international football tournament.

- Uruguay has won the tournament the most times—fifteen titles—followed by Argentina with fourteen titles; shockingly, Brazil has managed to win only eight times.
- The tournament's field consists of the ten national teams that are members of CONMEBOL (South American Football Confederation). Teams include Uruguay, Bolivia, Brazil, Chile, Colombia, Ecuador, Paraguay, Peru, Argentina, and Venezuela—two additional national teams are invited to participate in the event. The United States is the only non-CONMEBOL member to host, which they did in 2016.
- Two of the greatest South American players of all time were never able to win the highest regional honor, Pele and Diego Maradona. While Pele was still playing, Brazil could never lift the Copa América trophy, thanks to the likes of Argentina, Peru, and Uruguay. To add salt to the wound, during Pele's best years as a footballer, the tournament took a long eight-year break from 1967 to 1975.
- Norberto Mendez of Argentina and Zizinho of Brazil are the all-time leading scorers of Copa América, with seventeen goals for each to date.
- The Copa América trophy is more than one hundred years old. Unlike the first World Cup trophy, the Copa América trophy has been kept safe from the hands of robbers, so this vintage trophy has been embraced by the best players from different eras.
- A game to forget: Ecuadorian fans don't like to remember what happened on January 22, 1942, as they suffered a 0–12 defeat against Argentina, a record scoreline in Copa América history.
- Win-smin . . . who really needs a win anyway? In the 2011 Copa América, Paraguay managed to do something no other team ever could: they managed to sneak into the finals without winning a single game. They drew all three matches

in the group phase before winning the quarterfinal and the semifinal on penalties to seal a place in the final, where they ultimately lost to Uruguay.

- Martin Palermo took missing penalties to another level in the 1999 Copa América. In a game that Argentina eventually lost 3–0 to Colombia, Palermo missed not one, not two, but three penalties in a match that surely still haunts him to this day.

UEFA Championship

The UEFA, Union of European Football Associations, or Champions League, is the biggest stage for Europe's elite soccer clubs. Over the years, Spain has dominated the UEFA tournament with Real Madrid, led by Cristiano Ronaldo, as the most successful club in the tournament's history. In America, we are passionate about our baseball and football and many teams have dedicated superfans, but European soccer—sorry, futbol—fans take their passion for their clubs to another, sometimes dangerous level, as you'll read about below. In creating the cocktail Fernet About It!, my goal was to incorporate popular ingredients in Europe, such as Fernet-Branca, Italian sweet vermouth, and Bombay gin. As I mentioned earlier, Ronaldo played a major role in Real Madrid's success, and his recent move to Juventus has sparked renewed hope for the Italian club.

Fernet About It!

1 ½ oz. Bombay gin
½ oz. Pimm's No. 1
½ oz. sweet vermouth
¼ oz. Fernet-Branca
2 dashes orange bitters
1 dash Angostura bitters
Juice of 1 lemon wedge.

Here's How In a mixing glass with ice, combine all ingredients. Shake well and strain into a coupe glass. Garnish with orange twist.

How 'Bout That!

- The Union of European Football Associations (UEFA) is contested by top-division European clubs, deciding the best team in Europe. The pre-1992 competition was initially a straight knockout tournament open only to the champion club of each country.

- Introduced in 1992, the competition replaced the European Champion Clubs' Cup, or just European Cup, which had run since 1955. A group stage was added to the competition, and multiple entrants were allowed from certain countries.

- Real winners: The most successful club in the tournament's history is Real Madrid, who secured their thirteenth victory defeating Liverpool 3–1 in the 2018 finals. The highest number of victories according to countries is owned by Spanish clubs, with eighteen wins.

- Cristiano Ronaldo became the first player to score a goal in three UEFA finals: in 2008 for Manchester United and in 2014 and 2017 for Real Madrid. Ronaldo set a new record for a UEFA Champions League group stage with eleven goals in 2015–2016, eclipsing his own mark of nine in 2013–2014.

- Futbol gets the Royal treatment: UEFA commissioned Britain in 1992 to arrange an anthem, and the piece was performed by London's Royal Philharmonic Orchestra and sung by the Academy of St Martin in the Fields. The chorus contains the three official languages used by UEFA: German, English and French. The anthem's chorus is played before each UEFA Champions League game, as well as at the beginning and end of television broadcasts of the matches.

- Liverfools: English clubs were banned from the UEFA Champions League between 1986 and 1991 because of series of hooliganism and stadium disasters. The ban followed the death of thirty-nine Italian and Belgian football fans at Brussels' Heysel Stadium in a riot caused by English football deviants at that year's European Cup final. Right before the start of the match, at 7:00 p.m., a group of Liverpool fans, drunk from a day spent at the bars in Brussels, charged after a group of Juventus fans. In the melee, a stadium wall collapsed, crushing spectators. Others were trampled in the ensuing rush to flee the stadium. In all, thirty-two Juventus fans were killed, as well as seven bystanders; hundreds of other people were injured in the mayhem. To avoid further rioting from the unruly crowd, the game went on as scheduled. Juventus won 1–0. Anyone care?

- Take that, Super Bowl! The UEFA Champions League final is the most watched annual sporting event in the world. The final of 2012–2013 that featured Borussia Dortmund versus Bayern Munich was aired in more than two hundred countries and had the highest TV rating so far, with 360 million TV viewers, which included a record of 21,610,000 viewers in Germany.

- Messi the Magician: Lionel Messi became the first player to score five goals in a match in Barcelona's 7–1 win against Bayer Leverkusen on March 7, 2012.

- UEFA retains the original trophy at all times, but any team that wins three times in a row or five years overall gets the right to retain a full-sized replica. Really, three in a row and they get a replica? This honor was earned by six clubs so far—Milan, Real Madrid, Liverpool, Ajax, Bayern Munich, and Barcelona. The trophy weighs 7.5 kilograms, which equals roughly seventeen footballs (soccer balls, for Americans).

8
Football

SUPER BOWL

The Big Game. Everything about Super Sunday, as it's often referred to, screams excess: excess hype, excess commercials, excess halftime performances, excess joy, excess sorrow. Super Bowl Sunday is a fantastic day—the Christmas of sporting events. One of my fondest memories from my childhood was my parents' Super Bowl parties when the adults would play touch football and drink from a keg in the side yard. When the

Big Game finally started, everyone gorged on potluck appetizers and delivery pizza as we watched in our basement. If there's one key element to a successful Super Bowl Sunday, it's the pregame festivities—that is, drinking early, which is why I created my spin on the Bloody Mary. Odds are, if you're hosting or even going to a Super Bowl party, veggie dip will be served, so why not include a few of these items in a delicious, heavily garnished cocktail. The Big Game deserves a loaded cocktail.

Hail Mary

1 ½ oz. chili or pepper vodka
4 oz. tomato juice
1 tsp. prepared horseradish
2–3 dashes garlic salt
Pinch of pepper
2–3 dashes celery salt
Cucumber (3 slices for muddling, garnish)
Parsley (garnish)
Olives (garnish)

<u>Here's How</u> In a mixing glass, muddle 2 slices of cucumber. Add rest of ingredients and roll shake (light shake) to incorporate and chill ingredients. Strain into a pint glass and garnish with cucumber spear, parsley, and olives.

How 'Bout That!

• On January 15, 1967, in the very first Super Bowl, the Green Bay Packers defeated the Kansas City Chiefs, 35–10, at the Los Angeles Memorial Coliseum.
• Rare company: Pete Carroll, Jimmy Johnson, and Barry Switzer are the only coaches to win both an NCAA championship and a Super Bowl.
• The Super Bowl, in an attempt to limit ticket fraud, only issues paper tickets to the game. Tickets to the first Super Bowl in 1967 cost, on average, six dollars, which was still

considered too pricey for the general public; the "outlandish" ticket prices resulted in thirty thousand empty seats. The price was a steal considering the average cost for a ticket to Super Bowl 50 was over $4,700.

• Permanent supremacy: The Lombardi Trophy, comprised of sterling silver, is created by Tiffany & Co., and the winning team gets to keep it forever. No take-backs on this one!

• Trophy husband: Pete Rozelle, the NFL commissioner in 1967, was in charge of finding a trophy for the AFC-NFC Championship Game. For him, the trophy had to be first class, so the only company he contacted was Tiffany & Co. Their design chief, a native of Switzerland, knew absolutely nothing of football. Rozelle bought a football at FAO Schwarz and put it on the design chief's table. As the designer ate his corn flakes that morning, all while staring at the football, he began cutting the empty cereal box to use as a base for the football to sit atop. The designer sketched his trophy idea for Rozelle on a cocktail napkin at lunch a few days later, and voila!—the Vince Lombardi Trophy design was born, the same design we use today.

• Call it in the air: Each Super Bowl gets its own unique coin crafted by the Highland Mint. The front of the coin features the Lombardi Trophy along with the helmets of the two teams competing.

• Why the Roman numerals? The numbering system for the Super Bowls is courtesy of Lamar Hunt, former owner of the Kansas City Chiefs. NFL officials wanted to avoid confusion because the championship game is actually played the year after the corresponding season has ended. Good thinkin', Lamar.

• No, halftime performers at the Super Bowl do not get paid. However, all their expenses are covered, which includes bodyguards, lighting, stagehands, etc.—pretty much anything that would cost anything is covered. Who needs cash when the exposure the performing artists get is priceless? Many people watch solely for the halftime show; this is not an exaggeration, as the halftime show often receives higher ratings than the game itself.

- Big game, big cars: As a perk of making it to the Super Bowl, every player in the game gets a loaner car to drive around during Super Bowl Week.

- Pricey television: As of 2017, Super Bowl ads cost advertisers about $5 million for thirty-second spots.

- Watch your back, Turkey Day: Super Bowl is the second-biggest eating day on the calendar year, only behind Thanksgiving: 120,000,000 pounds of avocado, 4,000,000 pizzas, and 50,000,000 cases of beer are devoured and poured down the throats of football fans every year. Oh, add 1.25 billion chicken wings . . . not a good day for the chickens.

- Plenty of balls to go around: Each team in the Super Bowl gets 108 footballs: 54 for practice and 54 for the actual game. Typically, 120 balls are used per side, the extra 12 on account of the toughest guys on the gridiron, the kickers (cough, cough).

- The famous Har-bowl. What are the chances of two brothers both battling their way to the Super Bowl to coach against one another? Not good, but the Harbaugh brothers, John of the Baltimore Ravens and Jim with the 49ers, met in 2013, with John's Ravens the victors.

NCAA National Championship Game

The Southeastern United States is college football. The SEC has dominated college football for decades, especially with Nick Saban's Alabama Crimson Tide winning six national titles in the 2000s alone, which brings their total title count to eighteen. Of course, other conferences and programs have had their periods of dominance as well, but the South lives and breathes football. Fans of college football either love or hate the Alabama football program, but there is no denying their dominance. Most people have heard of the drink the Alabama Slammer, and I wanted to create a new take on this classic that highlights some of the staples the South is known for: whiskey and sweet tea. With the addition of pear liqueur and sparkling lemonade to finish, the cocktail is light and refreshing, yet still packs a punch to help out with the pregame tailgate ritual college football is renowned for.

Tailgate Bate

1 oz. Southern Comfort
1 oz. sloe gin
1 oz. pear liqueur
¼ oz. fresh lemon juice
2 oz. sweet tea
Sanpellegrino Limonata (sparkling lemonade) (to top)
Lemon wheel (garnish)
Mint (garnish)

<u>Here's How</u> Add all ingredients to a mixing glass with ice. Shake well and strain into a highball glass. Top with Sanpellegrino Limonata and garnish with lemon wheel and mint.

How 'Bout That!

- The college football term "bowl" comes from the Rose Bowl Stadium, which is shaped like—you guessed it—a bowl! The Rose Bowl is considered the prototype for many football stadiums around the country.

- One bad Barry: In 1988, Oklahoma State running back Barry Sanders lit up the league with 2,628 rushing yards, setting the all-time single season record (an average of 238.9 yards per game). Tack on thirty-nine touchdowns, another record for a single season. All in all, not a bad year for Barry.

- Yale holds the NCAA record with eighteen National Championships, their last title coming in 1927, as they are in the midst of an apocalyptic drought.

- The poor kickers: Field goals were originally worth five points, but this was changed to four in 1904, then decreased again to three points in 1909.

- The forward pass first appeared in college football in 1906 as an attempt to increase scoring and reduce injuries.

- Members of the College Football Selection Committee include athletic directors, former coaches, and players, who serve on a staggered three-year term. After week nine of play, the Selection Committee gets to work ranking the top twenty-five teams on a weekly basis by comparing and voting the top teams into the rankings. Similar to the process of bidding to hold the Super Bowl in your city, cities interested in hosting the National Championship Game must also submit a bid. Thank God there is *zero* room for corruption under this practice.

- Semifinal playoff games rotate between the Sugar Bowl, Rose Bowl, Orange Bowl, Cotton Bowl, Peach Bowl, and Fiesta Bowl.

- God rest his drool: Before every home game, flowers are placed at the graves of every former Uga (the English bulldog mascot of the University of Georgia).

- In the 1940s, college bowl games included the Raisin Bowl, Salad Bowl, and Oil Bowl.

- Chief Osceola, the Florida State mascot who rides out and plants a flaming spear at midfield before each home game, has been approved by Florida's Seminole Indian Tribe.

- Maybe too intimidating? The Wisconsin Badgers used to have a real-life badger as their mascot, which was led around the sidelines on a leash during games. The animal proved to have too much "spirit" (too mean), and it was replaced with a costumed mascot in 1940.

- The orange and white team colors of the Tennessee Volunteers were chosen in 1891 to represent the daisies that grow on the campus.

NFL Draft

Forget the fantasy draft, the NFL Draft is the real deal—one long weekend in April when collegiate footballers' lives are changed forever. What started with humble beginnings in 1936 is now a televised spectacle with viewing parties taking place across the country. Hemingway famously created Death in the Afternoon, an absinthe and champagne cocktail that he recommended drinking five of at a sitting. Being drafted into the NFL, instantly going from no paycheck to millions of dollars, certainly calls for celebration. And what better way to celebrate than with a little of the ole' bubbly? Draft in the Evening plays off Hemingway's cocktail using champagne and absinthe, the supposedly hallucinogenic wormwood-based liquor, because what's more surreal than hearing your name called, walking on stage, and sliding on the jersey of your new NFL team? (P.S. The chemical component that's found in wormwood, thujone, is mostly evaporated in the distillation process, so that spinning of the room you may feel is not you hallucinating, but likely you feeling the effects of absinthe's high alcohol content.)

Draft in the Evening

¾ oz. falernum syrup
½ oz. Bombay gin
¼ oz. absinthe
Champagne

<u>Here's How</u> In a mixing glass with ice, combine falernum, gin, and absinthe. Shake well and strain into a champagne flute. Top with champagne.

How 'Bout That!

- In the 1930s, Steelers team owner Bert Bell, who would go on to become NFL commissioner, was sick of his team losing and pitched an idea that would aim to spread the wealth in the NFL: a draft of college players in which teams would pick based on the reverse order of finish from the year before. Bell: "Gentlemen, I've always had the theory that pro football is like a chain. The league is no stronger than its weakest link and I've been a weak link for so long that I should know. Every year the rich get richer and the poor get poorer. Four teams control the championships, the Giants and Redskins in the East, and the Bears and Packers in the West. Because they are successful, they keep attracting the best college players in the open market—which makes them successful. I propose a change." And what a change it was!

- Each of the thirty-two teams receives one pick in each of the seven rounds in the NFL Draft. In the first round, teams get ten minutes to make each pick. In the second round, the time between each selection drops to seven minutes. In Rounds 3–6, teams get only five minutes to make their picks. In Round 7, teams get just four minutes to choose.

• Odds are against number one: In the first sixty-nine drafts, only fifteen hall-of-famers were selected at number one. Six number one picks have quarterbacked their teams to a Super Bowl title: Joe Namath, Terry Bradshaw, Jim Plunkett, John Elway, Troy Aikman, Peyton Manning, and Eli Manning.

• Scheduling conflict: In the height of the NFL versus AFL battle of the 1960s, the NFL held its draft in December to get a jump on the upstart league.

• The NFL actually instituted a "babysitting policy" during those contentious years. Handlers were tasked with taking young talent away from their schools during the AFL draft so teams had no way to contact them. One such excursion had twenty-seven players staying in a hotel, unknown to AFL officials.

• A lightly regarded prospect coming out of college, Tom Brady was selected by the New England Patriots with the 199th overall pick in the sixth round of the 2000 NFL Draft. And ten Super Bowl appearances later. . .

• John Matuszak is the only number one overall draft pick in the history of the NFL to play for a school that currently does not have a football program. His alma mater, the University of Tampa, terminated the program the year after he was drafted by the Houston Oilers.

• Long before he became a TV personality, Ahmad Rashād was chosen fourth overall by the Minnesota Vikings in 1972.

- Up in smoke: In 1999, the New Orleans Saints traded the rest of their entire draft to the Redskins to take Ricky Williams fifth overall.

- Until the advent of free agency in 1993, a team that drafted a player could force him to play for that team as long as the team still wanted him—basically for his entire career.

- In 1944, the Philadelphia Eagles used their twentieth-round pick on Syracuse fullback Norm Michael but were unable to contact him because he'd enlisted in the US Army just after college. While flipping through his local paper, fifty-five years later, an elderly Michael saw a list of every Syracuse player selected by the NFL and learned he'd once been drafted. And the hits keep coming!

- In 2000, the New York Jets set the record for the most first-round draft picks of all time with four selections.

9
Auto Racing

DAYTONA 500

The Great American Race. The Daytona 500 is the pinnacle of NASCAR racing, and the pageantry and spectacle of this unrivaled race day in February is legendary. Celebrities from all across the country yearn for the opportunity to put on the shoes of Grand Marshal of the race and utter those famous four words: "Drivers, start your engines!" What a feeling of power that must be, even if it's purely ceremonial. NASCAR fans are passionate about their favorite driver(s), so I created a drink that personifies this dedication to *your* driver—and your disdain and often out-right hatred for other drivers that just happen to be competing against Your Man or Woman.

Screw Others' Drivers

1 ½ oz. peach vodka
4 oz. fresh squeezed orange juice
12 oz. Coors Light (or your favorite race-day light beer)
Peach wedge (garnish)

<u>Here's How</u> Add the peach vodka and orange juice to a Collins glass with ice. Stir well, then top with Coors Light (there will be leftover beer in the can that can be added as the drink goes down, quickly, which I promise it will). Garnish with peach wedge.

How 'Bout That!

- The Daytona 500, or the Great American Race, as it has come to be known, covers five hundred miles and is two hundred laps long.
- Daytona International Speedway is the largest lighted sports facility in North America. More than two thousand lights have been installed around the track since the first night race in 1998.
- Beach cruisers: The Daytona Speedway we know today opened in 1959. Prior to this, races took place on the beach at what used to be the Daytona Beach Road Course.
- Richard Petty holds the record for most Daytona 500 victories with seven and was also in the first Daytona 500 with his dad, but Richard lost an engine early on in the race and finished in the back of the pack.
- Seventy-two-hour photo finish. The first Daytona 500 was held in 1959. The finish was so close that it took NASCAR three days to finally determine who won the race; it was Lee Petty.

- The Pontiac Trans-Am is the most-used Daytona 500 Pace Car, having made thirteen appearances in the Great American Race.

- A massive infield: Two full Disneylands would fit inside Daytona International Speedway's 180-acre infield.

- Daytona International Speedway houses the most stadium escalators of any outdoor stadium in the United States, with forty escalators and seventeen elevators.

- An estimated two hundred thousand gallons of beer is guzzled during the event, and the stench of stale beer goes hand in hand with the Daytona 500 and NASCAR as a whole. Residents in Daytona and surrounding areas complain about the smell, and residents as far south as Miami have reported being besieged by the boozy odor.

- Slow her on down, partner: In 1987, during his qualifying run for the Daytona 500, Ford driver Bill Elliott blistered around the track with a lap of 42.78 seconds with an average speed of 210.36 miles per hour. In response, NASCAR instituted the restrictor plate rule at Daytona with the intention of reducing horsepower to slow the speed.

- Pricey bodywork: If you'd like your company's logo on your favorite NASCAR driver's whip, it's going to cost you. Passing billboards at two hundred miles per hour are not cheap. In fact, Farmers Insurance paid $67.28 million to Hendrick Motorsports for their deal with Kasey Kahne. The company—again, Farmers—has paid roughly $660,000 per race over the past six seasons.

INDIANAPOLIS 500

Winning the Indy 500 is every Formula 1 driver's dream. Even if you aren't a fan of auto racing in general, odds are you've heard of and have a general idea of the importance of this race. Two hundred fifty thousand fans watch as the best drivers on the planet careen around the speedway at average speeds of upwards of 180 miles per hour. Prior to actually tuning in to watch an Indy 500, I'd heard about the "Brickyard" and the tradition of the winning driver chugging milk after their big win. The Brickyard Toast uses milk and espresso vodka as an ode to this finish line tradition and the adrenaline and speed show the drivers put on.

The Brickyard Toast

2 oz. espresso vodka
½ oz. Drambuie
¼ oz. Frangelico
1 ½ oz. whole milk
3 espresso beans (garnish)

<u>Here's How</u> Combine all ingredients in a mixing glass with ice and shake. Strain into a coupe glass. Garnish with 3 espresso beans.

How 'Bout That!

- The Indianapolis Motor Speedway is the world's largest spectator sporting facility, with more than 250,000 permanent seats. The speedway spans 253 acres and includes a golf course. The track publicity department would like to emphasize that Churchill Downs, Yankee Stadium, the Rose Bowl, the Roman Colosseum, and Vatican City can all fit inside the speedway, together.
- Speed Town, USA! By 1926, the track had spawned such a booming industrial economy that a residential neighborhood called Speedway, Indiana, was created near the event. The town is now home to some twelve thousand people and includes four elementary schools named after Indianapolis Motor Speedway's four original founders: James A. Allison, Carl G. Fisher, Arthur C. Newby, and Frank H. Wheeler.

- Saving face: The winner of the Indy 500 is awarded the sterling silver Borg-Warner Trophy, commissioned in 1935 at a cost of $10,000. Today, the trophy is worth more than $1 million. Winners of the Indy 500 don't just get their names inscribed on the race's trophy, they also get their likenesses permanently sculpted onto its sterling silver base.

- Although Danica Patrick was not the first female driver to compete in the Indy 500— that title was claimed by Janet Guthrie in 1977—she is somewhat of an Indy 500 legend on account of the records she broke, which include the record for having the highest starting place of any woman, the highest finishing place of any woman, more laps completed in a single race than any other woman, more laps completed in her career than any other woman, most laps led in a single race than any other woman, more laps led in her career than any other woman, more races finished running than any other woman, and more winnings than any other woman who has competed in the race.

- The Brickyard gets its name from the 1909 surfacing project when 3.2 million street paving bricks were laid on what became the Indianapolis Motor Speedway. The bricks were then covered over with asphalt. On the current asphalt track, one yard of the historic brickwork is exposed at the start-finish line.

- On May 30, 1911, the first Indy 500—originally called the International Sweepstakes—was won by Ray Harroun at an average speed of 74.602 miles per hour.

- Shotgun! During the early days of the Indy 500, nearly all the cars were two-seat setups that included a driver and an onboard riding mechanic. While the wheelman negotiated the track's four treacherous turns, the mechanic monitored gauges and tire wear, made on-the-fly repairs, and served as a traffic spotter. Sometimes they'd even massage the driver's aching arms and neck as the race wore on. Riding mechanics were mandatory at the Indy 500 from 1912 to 1922 and 1930 to 1937, but teams later abandoned two-man cars after World War II to cut down on weight and improve aerodynamics.

- Deadly Speed: In part to Indianapolis Motor Speedway's unforgiving corners and average speeds in excess of 180 miles per hour, the five-hundred-mile race has earned a reputation as one of the deadliest competitions in motorsports. Riding mechanic Sam Dickson became the first fatality after he was thrown into a fence during a crash in the inaugural 1911 race. Since 1911, some sixty drivers, mechanics, and spectators have died as a result of on-track accidents and debris.

- In May 1913, French-born rookie driver Jules Goux cruised to victory in the Indianapolis 500 by a ridiculous margin of over thirteen minutes, which included several pit stops, during which Goux not only tanked up on gas, but also refreshed himself with chilled champagne. Gotta love the French.

• What's with the milk? After becoming the Indy 500's first three-time winner in 1936, driver Louis Meyer famously chugged his favorite drink: a bottle of chilled buttermilk. He drank buttermilk because his mother advised him it was a good drink for a hot day. A milk industry executive saw a photograph of the celebration and arranged to have future winners repeat it, and it wasn't long before milk became a mainstay in the Indy 500's victory lane. Today, the American Dairy Association even asks drivers ahead of time whether they prefer whole, 2 percent, or skim milk in the event that they win the race. Fans don't appreciate when drivers try to break from the milk tradition, and when Brazilian driver Emerson Fittipaldi rebelled and drank orange juice following his 1993 victory, he was booed by spectators.

Monaco Grand Prix

Monaco is the land of lavish excess, wealth, and, of course, the Monaco Grand Prix, which runs through the city streets of the principality every year. For many, the race is an afterthought as mega-wealthy yacht owners park their vessels in the Mediterranean to get a glimpse of the wheeled bullets whizzing by through the streets. Midnight in Monaco is like Monaco itself in that if you're there, you're likely on vacation, and what pairs better with vacation than tropical ingredients like rum, pineapple juice, and coconut? Once the actual race ends, the party is just getting started!

Midnight in Monaco

1 ½ oz. vodka
½ oz. lightly aged rum
½ oz. crème de cacao
½ oz. fresh pineapple juice
2 dashes orange bitters
Coconut milk (to top)
Pineapple wedge (garnish)

<u>Here's How</u> Add all ingredients, except coconut milk, to a mixing glass with ice. Shake well and strain into a martini glass. Float coconut milk on top, and garnish with fresh pineapple wedge.

How 'Bout That!

- The Monaco Grand Prix, along with the Singapore Grand Prix, is a street circuit, meaning the race takes place on real public roads that have been closed to the public and are lined with unforgiving barriers.

- At just over two miles long, the Monaco Grand Prix has the shortest track on the F1 calendar. However, its seventy-eight laps are the most of any circuit. The Monaco Grand Prix circuit boasts the slowest corner—Turn 6—in Formula 1 racing. The event is unique in that each race has been held on the same circuit—the streets of the principality—for years. The only other circuit that compares is the Italian Grand Prix at Autodromo Nazionale Monza.

- Brazilian racing car driver Nelson Piquet famously compared driving at Monaco to "riding a bicycle around your living room." It is the most technically demanding race and the ultimate test of a driver's skill. By the time they reach the finish line, a driver will make almost five thousand gear changes.

- Monaco is a constitutional monarchy with Prince Albert II as head of state. One of only three sovereign city-states in the world, alongside Vatican City and Singapore, the tiny tax haven on the Mediterranean coast measures just 0.78 square miles and is home to 38,000 high-net-worth individuals, including many current and past F1 drivers.

- Ayrton Senna is the current record holder for number of Monaco Grand Prix wins. His six victories are impressive, while Graham Hill and Michael Schumacher have bagged five each.

- The MGP was first staged in 1929 on a layout of the circuit very similar to the one used today. The race was organized by a wealthy tobacco manufacturer, Antony Noghès, who had set up the Automobile Club de Monaco with some of his friends. It wasn't until Jackie Stewart's safety campaign in the late 1960s and early 1970s that modifications were made to the circuit to improve safety, such as the addition of Armco barriers.

- Each year, more than twenty miles of safety rails are erected. This is on top of 3,600 tires for tire barriers and 215,000 square feet of wire catch fencing, which is understandable when you need to turn a city into a full-blown race circuit.

- The Monaco Grand Prix is part of the Triple Crown of Motorsport achievement. Along with the Indianapolis 500 and 24 Hours of Le Mans, it's one of the world's three most prestigious F1 motor races that a driver can win in their career.

- Won if by land; two in the sea: Only two cars have ever ended up in the Mediterranean Sea as a result of the Monaco Grand Prix. Alberto Ascari and Paul Hawkins were the two drivers who had their backs to the racetrack as they crashed into the water.

- In 2004, to promote the blockbuster film *Ocean's Twelve*, the Jaguar team ran a special livery at the Monaco Grand Prix, complete with precious diamonds attached to the nose cones of the cars. Turns out diamonds aren't forever. On lap one, the Jaguar of Christian Klien hit the barriers and retired from the race. The team couldn't recover the car or even examine the crash site until the race finished two hours later. Surprise, surprise, the $300,000 diamonds were nowhere to be seen! "That will be the most expensive drive I'll ever take around Monte Carlo," said Klien after the race.

- Tough road: Monaco holds the record in the modern F1 era for the least number of cars to finish a race—only four cars made it to the checkered flag in both 1966 and 1996.
- Party time: The rich and famous make room in their calendars for the weekend of exclusive parties and celebrations that accompanies the Monaco Grand Prix. The race weekend is often combined with the Cannes Film Festival, which finishes during the preceding week, as the superrich cruise into the harbor to watch the race unfold from their superyachts. Not a bad life.

10
Action Sports

FIS Alpine Skiing World Cup

Growing up in southwest Virginia, I was fortunate to have an expat French-Canadian father who traveled south to Virginia to play hockey and exposed me to the world of alpine skiing in the process. The sport of alpine skiing opens up an unknown world of snowcapped towering peaks and vast slopes perfect for carving your way down. If you've ever watched a downhill race on TV, you have an idea of the incredible athleticism and leg strength these athletes must have to career down a mountain at upwards of eighty to ninety miles per hour on what is essentially ice—not to mention the level of insanity required and ability to mentally shut out the very real possibility of a horrific crash. I created a cocktail to reflect the après-ski culture, a refreshing drink to take the edge off after or before you're done edging down the slopes or just watching these incredible skiers on TV from the safety of your couch.

Snowmelt

1 oz. amaretto
½ oz. white crème de cacao
1 ½ oz. cream
Orange (wedge for muddling, spiral for garnish)

<u>Here's How</u> Muddle orange wedge in mixing glass. Add ice and add all other ingredients. Shake well and strain into coupe glass. Garnish with orange spiral.

How 'Bout That!

• The International Ski Federation (FIS) is the world governing body of alpine skiing. The organization first recognized downhill ski racing in 1930. The first world championships for men's downhill and slalom events took place in 1931. In 1950, women's events were added, and the racer with the most overall points at the end of the season takes home the overall World Cup Title.

• The word "ski" comes from the Old Norse word *skíð*, meaning stick of wood.

• There's got to be a better way! After the last ice age, Stone Age hunters started strapping long pieces of wood to their feet in an attempt to more efficiently pursue game that thrived across Europe and Asia. Modern skiing has evolved from origins in Scandinavia. However, ten-thousand-year-old wall paintings suggest skis were used in the Xinjiang area of what is now China.

• "Skiing" is the only six-letter word in the English language with a double i exactly in the middle.

• Mystery solved of skiing's popularity in Switzerland: Sir Arthur Conan Doyle, known as the creator of Sherlock Holmes, helped to make skiing popular in Switzerland. Knowing Switzerland has the perfect terrain for skiing, he brought back skis with him after a ski trip to Norway. The Swiss took to the novel sticks of wood.

• Downhill GOAT Franz Klammer is regarded as the best downhill skier of all time. Although he never won the World Cup, the Austrian won the downhill title five times and has twenty-six World Cup wins to his credit, along with an Olympic gold in 1976.

• Lindsey Vonn is the most decorated female skier of all time. She has won seventy-eight World Cup events and has won the overall World Cup championship four times. She won three individual Olympic medals, one of which was gold, and four team Olympic medals along with her US teammates—all of these accolades despite the fact that she hates the cold weather.

• Today, competitive alpine skiing is divided into four races: slalom, giant slalom, super giant slalom (super-G), and downhill. The events get progressively faster and have fewer and fewer turns, as evidenced by the extreme downhill event.

• Around 400 million people ski annually, and there are nearly two thousand alpine skiing areas in the world. Europe dominates the ski market with some 200 million skiers per year, with the United States ranking as the second-largest market with about 80 million taking to the slopes per year.

• Nick Willey of Australia holds the record for the longest time spent skiing nonstop at 202 hours, 1 minute. He accomplished the feat(?) at Thredbo, New South Wales, Australia, in 2005. He traveled more than 715 miles in the process, skiing down the slopes 916 times. When asked to comment, Willey was asleep.

• Life and death in the fast lane: The first Olympic downhill race was held in Switzerland in 1948 and was won by Henri Oreiller, who had a reputation for being a cocky skier who careened down courses like an acrobat. He was also a member of the French Underground in World War II. The thrill of skiing at breakneck speeds was apparently not enough, and he turned to race car driving and was killed at thirty-six years old behind the wheel of his Ferrari in 1962.

• World Cup and Olympic champion skier Mikaela Shiffrin was born on March 13, 1995, in Vail, Colorado. She competed in her first international competition at age fifteen and became the youngest ever to win an Olympic gold medal in the slalom. She skis with the initialism ASFTTB on her helmet and skis, which stands for "Always Ski Faster than the Boys."

- FIS has broadened its categories and is recognizing other sports such as speed skiing, grass skiing—skiing on grass using a type of skate rather than a ski—and telemark skiing, in which a skier's heel is not locked down and is free to move up and down, similar to a cross-country motion.

SUMMER X GAMES

What started as simply a showcase for alternative sports has exploded into the X Games, an annual competition that combines athleticism with some of the most daring and dangerous tricks ever attempted in competition. I fell in love with the X Games when I was in high school and thought that I wanted to be a professional stuntman (which didn't quite pan out). Long before Shaun White took over the torch as the X Games' leading man, Tony Hawk paved the way for athletes around the world as the unofficial ambassador of the Summer X Games. Not only did Hawk excel at advancing the X Games, but he also flourished when he wasn't competing by launching Birdhouse, his skateboarding company, a video game series, and countless advertisements, proving that you don't have to be a mainstream sports star to make a career out of the sports you love. Oh, and who could forget the magic he created when he became the first skateboarder to successfully land the 900 in the halfpipe? In honor of Mr. Hawk and his contributions to the world of X Games, I created Skyhawk, a perfect cocktail for sipping while watching the baddest men and women on the planet defy gravity at the Summer X Games.

Skyhawk

1 ½ oz. peach vodka
½ oz. mezcal
¼ oz. blue curaçao
½ oz. fresh lime juice
½ oz. simple syrup
1 oz. fresh orange juice
Orange wheel (garnish)

<u>Here's How</u> In a mixing glass with ice, add all ingredients. Shake well and strain into a coupe glass. Garnish with orange wedge resting on the rim of the cocktail.

How 'Bout That!

- The ESPN Extreme Games, originally envisioned as a biannual showcase for "alternative" sports, were first held June 24–July 1, 1995, in Newport, Rhode Island. The success of the inaugural event prompted organizers to make it an annual competition. Now, athletes compete in twenty-seven events in nine sport categories: eco-challenge, bungee jumping, inline skating, skateboarding, skysurfing, sport climbing, street luge, biking, and water sports. One hundred ninety-eight thousand spectators attended the first Extreme Games. Seven sponsors, including Advil, Mountain Dew, Taco Bell, AT&T, Chevy Trucks, Nike, and Miller Lite Ice, lend their support to the event.
- The name X Games was decided in the second year.
- We could be heroes: The X Games competitions offers a stage to shine for athletes who are talented and brave enough to pull off new and exciting tricks, such as Tony Hawk's 900 in skateboarding, Travis Pastrana's double backflip in freestyle motocross, Heath Frisby's first snowmobile front flip, and snowboarder Torstein Horgmo's triple flip.

• After eleven attempts, Tony Hawk nailed the first-ever 900 in competition in Vert Best Trick at X Games 5 in San Francisco. Hawk, skateboarding's mainstream ambassador, is a major icon and licensed a line of successful video games along with his skateboarding company, Birdhouse.

• The regulars: Bob Burnquist, Rune Glifberg, Andy Macdonald, and Dennis McCoy have competed in all seventeen X Games.

• Communication is key: When you host events that are dangerous in nature and require constant communication among those telling competitors when to start or end an event, radios are key, which is why 73 two-way radio channels are dedicated to the event.

• BMX and skateboard are the only two sports that have been in the X Games since 1995. Dave Mirra has won the most medals in X Games history. He won a total of twenty-four medals. Mirra's life ended in tragedy, as he took his own life with a shotgun. He was diagnosed posthumously with chronic traumatic encephalopathy (CTE), the disease most often associated with successive concussions.

RED BULL CLIFF DIVING

It's the worst nightmare for many of us, but for the incredible athletes that make a career out of cliff diving, it's a passion and thrill like no other. Divers travel around the world, voluntarily throwing themselves off platforms ninety feet above the water's surface. And they do so with a grace and beauty that has to be seen to be believed. What started as a small event in Arizona in 1999 has blossomed into a worldwide phenomenon with divers traveling to nine different locations—many exotic paradises—to wow the crowds that gather on the cliffsides and anchor their boats to get a great view of these courageous athletes teetering on the verge of serious injury, but also greatness. I created Crème de Cliff to be enjoyed with the spirit of summer and the tropical locations where divers often compete. When I think of water and the oceans these men and women torpedo into, I immediately think of watermelon and coconuts and the warmth of summer.

Crème de Cliff

1 oz. lavender-infused gin
¾ oz. crème de violette
½ oz. crème de coconut
1 ½ oz. fresh watermelon puree
½ oz. fresh lemon juice
Watermelon wedge (garnish)

<u>Here's How</u> In a mixing glass with ice, add all ingredients. Shake well and strain into a coupe glass. Garnish with watermelon wedge.

How 'Bout That!

• Isn't there something else I could do for you, sir? Cook! I can cook for you! Cliff diving originated in eighteenth-century Maui, Hawaii. The king of Maui would demand his warriors jump feetfirst off of cliffs to prove their loyalty, fearlessness, and courage.

• Ninety-two—the height in feet of most diving platforms on the Cliff Diving World Series.

• Diving legend and four-time Olympic champion Greg Louganis is the sports director for Red Bull Cliff Diving.

• In 2019, Rhiannan Iffland, the unstoppable Australian cliff diver, enjoyed the type of year most athletes can only dream of after winning all seven Red Bull Cliff Diving stops to complete a historic perfect season and wrap up her fourth title in a row.

• The inaugural event was held in Lake Havasu, Arizona, in September 1999 and was titled On the Rocks. Eight divers from around the world participated. Ten years later, the Red Bull Cliff Diving World Series was born in France, which attracted thirty thousand spectators.

• Divers leap from almost three times the ten-meter Olympic height and hit the water at upwards of fifty miles per hour. It's imperative the divers enter the water "in form"—Barani—diving terminology which means the divers do one forward somersault rotation with a half twist. This is used as an entry maneuver to the water, and the skill must be mastered to be a successful cliff diver.

• The events always have scuba divers in the water below as a safety precaution. Safety divers also splash the water around so the divers above can visualize where the surface of the water is.

• In 2014, the women's diving world series was born. The women take off from sixty-eight-foot platforms, which is slightly lower because of female body builds and their ability to handle the impact of the water.

• There are around nine Red Bull Cliff Diving events taking place each year all around the world, each in breathtaking locations including the oceanside, a lake, the heart of a city, a historical landmark, and a quarry.

• Athletes train on platforms and dry gyms with foam to hone the muscle movement and muscle memory. Divers then piece together different aspects of the dive for the twenty-seven-meter freefall.

• Judges have three seconds to evaluate three parts of a dive, which include takeoff, position in the air, and water entry.

• A little more diving terminology: DD, degree of difficulty—a calculation based on the difficulty of the execution of each maneuver and the junction of each dive component. For me, DD would be "designated diver," because I'm not leaving that twenty-seven-meter platform.

• There are twenty-two possible number of figure combinations for men and seventeen for women: back, forward, inward or reverse, arm or back, flying, free or pike, from one to five somersaults, and half to five twists. Divers need a mix of three to four of these to get the combination they need to plan and perform when jumping off the diving board.

• The man, the myth, the legend: British diver Gary Hunt has thirty victories and made sixty podiums in his cliff-diving career.

I'm a huge fan of the Winter X Games. I grew up skiing and looking through ski magazines that were writing profile pieces on the young snowboarding phenomenon, Shaun White. White, the Flying Tomato, as he was known before he cut his flowing red locks, is the most decorated athlete in Winter X Games history. If you've watched Mr. White on the halfpipe, in the slopestyle event, or in the Olympics, you've most likely been amazed by his ability to rise to the occasion, no matter the pressure. My goal in creating Slopestyle Espress was to create a cocktail that could not only keep you alert and on your toes to watch the amazing athletes pull off unthinkable tricks, hence the espresso vodka, but also a drink that could be enjoyed on a cold winter day.

Slopestyle Espress

1 ½ oz. espresso vodka
1 oz. apricot brandy
1 oz. Cointreau
1 oz. cream
½ oz. blueberry simple syrup*
½ oz. fresh lemon juice
Blueberries (garnish)

*Blueberry simple syrup Combine 1 cup of water and 1 cup of granulated sugar in a saucepan over medium heat. Continue to stir until all sugar has dissolved. Add 1 cup of fresh blueberries and continue to simmer until blueberries are soft enough to mash. Mash and strain through a fine-mesh sieve. Let cool before using.

<u>Here's How</u> In a mixing glass, combine all ingredients. Shake well and strain over a single round ice cube in a rocks glass. Garnish with blueberries on cocktail spear.

How 'Bout That!

- In 1997, the first Winter X Games were held at Snow Summit Mountain Resort in Big Bear Lake, California, before moving to Crested Butte, Colorado, in 1998. Thirty-eight thousand spectators watched Sweden's Jennie Waara win three snowboarding medals to become the first, and still the only, competitor to win three medals in the same year. The games were broadcast in nearly two hundred countries, and many viewers got their first taste of competitive ice-climbing, snowboarding, and snow mountain bike racing.
- In 2015, a crowd of more than 115,000 people watched the games in Aspen over the four days.
- Tragedy in 2013: Snowmobiler Caleb Moore performed a flip and died after his snowmobile landed on him during the Best Trick competition. His death was on public display, and organizers decided to drop the event from future X Games.
- The 2011 Winter X Games was officially the most watched ever, with 114,200 spectators in attendance and a global television audience of more than 39 million viewers.
- ESPN introduced the use of drones for the first time in 2015 to capture incredible television pictures of athletes from the air.

- Snowboarder Jamie Anderson has amassed more Olympic and Winter X Games medals than any other female athlete in history. She wants her young fans to realize that even the greatest athletes sometimes fail and that it's how you respond that matters most.

- Admission to watch the events at Winter X Games is free, although fans can also purchase a music pass for $125.

- Quick tune-up: In 2002, only weeks before the Winter Olympics in Salt Lake City, the entire US Olympic Snowboard Freestyle Team showed up to compete in the Winter X snowboard superpipe event.

- High-Flying Tomato: Snowboarder Shaun White is the most decorated Winter X Games athlete in history, with sixteen medals—thirteen of which are gold. White is the only athlete to compete in both the Summer X Games and Winter X Games in two different disciplines.

- The Winter X Games have proved incredibly lucrative to the Buttermilk ski resort in the Aspen area. During the games, Fork Valley's hotels, lodges, and inns balloon to 98 percent occupancy. During previous games, Aspen's lodges have recorded sales of $21.1 million, and restaurants and bars saw $10.8 million in spending. Not a bad week.

- Move aside, Olympics: For over a century, winning a gold medal at the Winter Olympics was the highest honor an athlete could achieve. Today, the Winter Olympics struggles to keep up with the Winter X Games in attracting the younger demographic of eighteen- to thirty-four-year-olds. This is a big deal and a huge problem for the Winter Olympics—so big a problem, in fact, that they have started to introduce the "cooler" winter sports to their program, such as freestyle skiing and snowboarding.

Throughout middle and much of high school, my friends and I spent our days on our mountain bikes, peddling around town trying to find trails to hit and drops to, well, drop off of. I went as far as building a ramp to jump over my sister's Honda Accord, which, as crazy as it sounds, was successful! As you can imagine, I was thrilled to find the Red Bull Rampage event on TV. My biking antics in the backyard and on nearby trails pale in comparison to the insane lines and drops the competitors ride at Rampage. To simply make it down the course in one piece, slowly, would be a feat, but riders at Rampage take it to another level by backflipping off monstrous gaps or doing 360s off of dirt ramps on their lines down. There's always a certain amount of fear needed to compete at this level given the dangerous nature of the sport, but these athletes, in my mind, are as close to fearless as it comes, which is why I created Lions in Zion, a tribute to the courageous performances they put on every year at Rampage.

Lions in Zion

¾ oz. Disaronno Amaretto Liqueur
¾ oz. apricot brandy
¾ oz. Jack Daniels Honey
1 oz. tart cherry juice
½ oz. fresh lemon juice
Lemon peel (garnish)

<u>Here's How</u> In a mixing glass, combine all ingredients. Shake well and strain into a rocks glass over one large ice cube. Express lemon peel over drink to release the oil. Rub peel around rim of glass, then garnish on rim of the cocktail.

How 'Bout That!

• What exactly is Red Bull Rampage? Basically, it's a freeride mountain biking event where competitors peddle down a highly elevated, rugged mountainside by choosing the steepest lines and throwing in jaw-dropping tricks on their descent.

• Rules on the dirt: A rider is allowed a two-person crew to help them dig and create whatever features, jumps, or drops they want on the mountain over a four-day period. Competitors are allowed to use sandbags and digging equipment including shovels and rakes to build their lines. No power tools. Once the four-day building period is over, the riders have four days to practice riding and fine-tuning the lines they created. When competitors arrive at a Rampage venue, the mountain is typically in its raw, natural state—a blank, rocky canvas for the bikers to create the kind of course they want to ride. Past venues have had large, manufactured ramps and drops from which riders could do big tricks off, but this is no longer the case, as the organizers wanted to go back to the basics of freeriding. Today, riders carve their own lines and use natural features to build jumps, drops, and berms.

• The event is not timed, so it's not a race against the clock. Instead, riders have to impress the judges with their style, line choice, and airtime. There are three main criteria that judges use:

1. Line choice: The steeper and more difficult the line choice, the more points scored.
2. Airtime and tricks: The amplitude of the jumps, added tricks, and sticking the landings are things that will award the most points.
3. Fluidity, speed, and style: The smoother, faster, and more aggressive, the higher the final points will be.

• The now-iconic big-mountain freeride inaugural event was held near Utah's Zion National Park in 2001 with a field composed of freeride pioneers, dirt jumpers, and downhill racers. Rampage now offers hundreds of thousands of dollars in prize money, but the original competition had a total purse of just $8,000.

• From 2001 till 2004, Rampage was held off Kolob Terrace Road, on the western boundary of Zion National Park. The competition was held from 2001 to 2004, but then was canceled due to the increasing risk competitors were taking.

• No meeting the maker in Zion: Despite the frightening terrain and gravity-defying tricks riders perform, there have been no deaths in Rampage's twelve-year history. There have, however, been cringe-inducing crashes and potentially career-ending injuries. As rider Darren Berrecloth puts it, "You're really just trying to avoid dying—some cliffs are fine, you'll get beat up a bit, but other ones can really hurt you."

• But first, a mountain bike audition: Rampage is not a course on which riders try new tricks. Potential competitors—who come from freestyle, downhill, and freeride mountain biking—must submit video proof of their riding experience on similar terrain to be invited by the promoter. If a rider doesn't have the chops to back up their application, they can't compete.

11
Basketball

NCAA March Madness

March is the time when any and every team has the opportunity to win a National Championship in college basketball—assuming they made the tournament, of course. It's do or die, win or go home—cut-and-dried. The blue-chip programs—Duke, UNC, Kansas, Kentucky, etc.—all have targets on their backs from nationally unknown schools that may be competing in the tournament for the first time in their program's history. And all it takes is one win to move on. Every program in the tournament, no matter how large and distinguished, or small and unknown, has its shot at glory. I personally root for the Cinderella story, the team that wasn't supposed to make the tournament in the first place and surely wasn't supposed to win once there. In the spirit of the underdog in the March Madness tournament, I created Cinderella's Sipper, a light in body and texture cocktail that despite its airy and unassuming appearance, can sneak up on you with its underlying strength.

Cinderella's Sipper

1 ½ oz. vanilla vodka
1 oz. crème de violette
½ oz. simple syrup
½ oz. fresh lemon juice
¼ oz. blue curaçao
Lemon twist (garnish)

<u>Here's How</u> Add all ingredients into a mixing glass. Add ice and shake. Strain into a coupe glass and garnish with lemon twist cut to resemble a slipper.

How 'Bout That!

- If you're tired of all the naysayers telling you your bracket is hopeless, then don't read the following statistic: the odds of filling out a perfect bracket are 1 in 9,223,372,036,854,775,808 (that's quintillion, Doug from Florida, who's "feeling good" about his bracket this year).
- Time well spent: Up to 20 percent of Americans fill out brackets in any given year, resulting in millions of distracted workers. According to *US News & World Report*, $4 billion is lost in productivity. Yeah, but did you see that buzzer beater!?
- UCLA head coach John Wooden has the most National Championships with ten.

- Go big, or you can't host: Final Four arenas must, by NCAA mandate, hold at least a seventy-thousand-seat capacity.

- The most common upset in the tournament has been a number twelve seed over a number five seed.

- Villanova, the number eight seed, was the lowest seed to win the tournament. They accomplished the feat in 1985.

- The Tennessee Lady Vols have never missed a NCAA tournament. They've competed in the NCAA Women's Division I Tournament every year since its 1982 inauguration.

- Indy is home, at least periodically: It is an actual official NCAA rule that the Final Four take place in Indianapolis every five years. Indy is the home of the NCAA headquarters.

- No matter the sex: In 2004, the Connecticut Huskies became the only school to win his-and-her national championships in the same year. The Husky dominance was no fluke, as both teams accomplished the feat again in 2014.

- Greatest disappointment of all time: This dubious honor belongs to the Virginia Cavaliers, who came into the 2018 tournament as the number one seed and were ousted in the first round by number sixteen seed UMBC–University of Maryland Baltimore County in the greatest upset in NCAA tournament history. But wait, vindictive Virginia returned in the 2019 tournament and won it all, beating Texas Tech in the championship game to thoroughly right the wrongs of the previous season.

- Hell, take the floor as well! We've all seen the tournament champions cut down the net after their final win, but since 1986, the winning team has also been given the hardwood court to auction off or sell pieces of hardcourt history to fans.

- Sweetie, I think I will have that procedure now: The number of vasectomy procedures performed on men increases exponentially in advance of March Madness, which is no coincidence. The thought of going under the knife is eased somewhat by the thought of three days of guilt-free binge watching of the tournament while posted up on an inflatable doughnut. Throw a few beers in there as incentive, and men would be willing to make the procedure an annual event: vasectomy, reversal, vasectomy, reversal.

- The University of Connecticut women's basketball program holds the record for most consecutive victories with 111.

NBA FINALS

The NBA Finals is filled with high drama. From Lebron James leading his Cavaliers over the hump and out of the drought against the Warriors to all of Jordan's heroics and dominance with the Bulls, the battle for NBA supremacy rarely disappoints. The game has come a long way since James Naismith's original invention of basketball in the late 1900s. What I truly enjoy about the NBA and all the teams battling for the title is that it is everchanging with new teams emerging to compete, thanks to a few good trades here and there. Yes, the Western Conference has dominated the scene for the past decade, but the Eastern Conference is, again, only a few moves and great players away from working itself back into contention.

Buzzer Beater

1 ½ oz. brandy
½ oz. Drambuie
2 oz. fresh pineapple juice
¼ oz. brown sugar simple syrup
¼ oz. fresh lemon juice
Brown sugar (garnish for rim of glass)
Pineapple wedge (Garnish)

<u>Here's How</u> Using juice from lemon wedge, line the rim of the glass, then roll the glass in sugar. Add all ingredients to a shaker with ice. Shake well and strain into a coupe glass and garnish with pineapple wedge.

How 'Bout That!

• The King and his court: During the 2016 NBA Finals, Lebron James led his Cavaliers and all players on both the Cavaliers and Warriors in points, rebounds, steals, assists, and blocks in the series. Lebron is the only player in NBA history to lead all players in the five categories for an entire playoff series.

• Bobbing for rotten apples: In 2012, the Charlotte Bobcats ended their season with a record of seven wins and fifty-nine losses, giving them the worst season in history. What's the pep talk at the end of that season? It's only up from here, fellas?

- Five-time NBA champ Kobe Bryant wasn't even a top-ten pick in the draft coming out of high school. Despite being a dominant high school stud, he dropped to the thirteenth pick. Bryant's middle name is Bean, after his father, Joe "Jellybean" Bryant.

- One and done: Wilt Chamberlain spent just one year with the Harlem Globetrotters, but his impression was certainly felt, as they retired his number 13 jersey. His signature trick while with the Globetrotters was picking up Captain Meadowlark Lemon off of the ground and throwing him high in the air before catching him.

- Jump balls in the NBA used to be after every basket.

- Despite what many may believe, or want to believe, Michael Jordan was not the first overall pick in the NBA draft. MJ was selected third, just behind hall-of-famer Hakeem Olajuwon and Sam Bowie.

- Cities holding their ground: The Celtics and Knicks are the only NBA teams to have never moved—every other original team has either folded or moved since the league's inception.

- Lebron James, believe it or not, was not the first highly advertised high school prospect to play in the NBA. Moses Malone owns this honor; as a center and forward, Malone spent nineteen years in the NBA and had a stellar career despite never playing in college.

- In 1891, James Naismith, a PE teacher from Canada, invented the game of basketball for his gym class at the YMCA school in Springfield, Massachusetts. The goal was to create a sport to play indoors, sheltered from the harsh weather. The game started with soccer balls being thrown into wooden peach baskets that were attached to balconies at opposite ends of the court. The baskets had bottoms, so the officials had to climb a ladder each time a team made a shot. This may also have been the time period when poor sportsmanship was invented, as officials likely screamed at shooting players in the hopes they'd miss and they wouldn't have to climb the damn ladder again.

• Little man, big dreams: Muggsy Bogues, at five feet, three inches, is the smallest player ever to play in the NBA, and he wasn't a big star in college playing at Wake Forest. Despite his average numbers and subaverage height, Bogues was drafted in the first round and went on to have a fourteen-year career in the NBA, securing his job as a defensive threat and solid passer.

• The last buzzer beater in the NBA Finals was Game 1 in 1997 by Michael Jordan.

• Lord of the rings: Bill Russell has won eleven NBA Championship rings, all with the Boston Celtics. He's tied with Henri Richard of the NHL for the most championships won by a single player. Just to add a little icing on his illustrious cake, Russell is one of only seven players who has won an NCAA, NBA Championship, and Olympic Gold Medal.

NBA All-Star Game & Skills Competition

Michael Jordan, Vince Carter, Kobe Bryant . . . Spud Webb? The Slam Dunk Contest at the NBA All-Star Weekend is by far the most thrilling event. Yes, the Three-Point Shootout is nice too, and the actual game is fun to watch as long as you're not a fan of defense. Although it was way back in 1986, the Atlanta Hawks' five-foot-seven Spud Webb stole the show, and the trophy, from teammate Dominique Wilkins after demonstrating incredible hops for a lil' guy. In honor of Spud and his takeover of the 1986 Slam Dunk Contest, I incorporated vodka, a Russian staple, as a way to play on Sputnik, the first artificial satellite launched into orbit. If you've seen Spud Webb's vertical jump, you've seen a small man leaping out of this world. The cocktail uses fresh peach puree as an ode to the Atlanta Hawks and Georgia, a state known for its peaches and given the moniker the Peach State.

Spudnick

2 oz. peach vodka
1 ½ oz. fresh peach puree
½ oz. simple syrup
2 dashes vanilla extract
Cream (to float)

<u>Here's How</u> In a mixing glass with ice, add all ingredients except the cream. Shake well and strain into a coupe glass. Using the backside of a barspoon, pour cream over the spoon into the cocktail. Using the opposite end of the barspoon, lightly stir cream to incorporate.

How 'Bout That!

- Starting players are chosen by votes cast by fans, players, and members of the media. Team captains are the top winners of fan votes in each conference. The two captains select their teams from the pool of All-Stars. Under the new format, the teams will still feature twelve players from each conference, but captains can select from either conference. Reserves, seven from each conference, are selected by the NBA's head coaches, and head coaches for the All-Star teams are based on the teams with the best records in each conference two weeks prior to the All-Star Game.
- The first All-Star Game took place on March 2, 1951, at the Boston Garden. The East won 111–94, and Ed Macauley was named the MVP.
- The Slam Dunk Contest debuted in 1976 during halftime of the All-Star Game, laying the foundation for the modern-day All-Star Weekend. Julius Erving was named the winner.

• Little man, giant hops: The Slam Dunk Contest has given rise to some of the NBA's smallest players, including in 1986 when five-foot-seven Spud Webb defeated his Hawks teammate and defending champion Dominique Wilkins. Webb is still to this day the shortest player to win the event, but five-foot-nine Nate Robinson has the most contest titles with three. Spud was actually instrumental in coaching and supporting Robinson in his pursuit of the Slam Dunk titles.

• Quite a kid! The youngest NBA All-Star starter was nineteen-year-old Kobe Bryant in 1998. Kobe Bryant also holds the record for youngest player to win the Slam Dunk Contest, at age eighteen. Not to be outdone by Kobe, twenty-one-year-old Lebron James became the youngest player to be named All-Star Game MVP in 2006.

• On July 22, 2016, the NBA announced they would move the 2017 All-Star Game from Charlotte, North Carolina, to New Orleans, Louisiana, because of state legislation passed in March that limited anti-discrimination protections for LGBT people and demands that transgender people use the bathroom according to the gender on their birth certificate. However, the NBA later announced the 2019 All-Star Game would be played in Charlotte, citing the partial repeal of the so-called Bathroom Bill as the reason for the change. Smart thinking, Charlotte officials . . .

• Magical selection: In 1992, just months after announcing that he was HIV positive, Earvin "Magic" Johnson was voted into the All-Star Game—oh, and was also named MVP— despite not playing all season.

• Larry Bird was the inaugural winner of the Three-Point Shooting Contest. He, along with Craig Hodges, have each won three consecutive times.

• Everything's bigger in Texas: The most attended NBA All-Star Game was held at Cowboys Stadium in 2010 before an astounding 108,713 spectators.

12
Combat Sports

BOXING HEAVYWEIGHT CHAMPIONSHIP OF THE WORLD

Boxing may have lost some of its popularity after the public "suddenly" realized that pounding on each other's skulls and rattling brains was not exactly safe, but the heavyweight title of the world is still an impressive feat. Sure, we may not have the household names of Tyson, Holyfield, Foreman, Ali, or Frasier, but the sport is still alive and well. Although the sport of boxing may be in its trough phase, it will likely crest again. Boxing is full of skillfully devised combinations, which is why I use sloe gin—made from the sloe berry—and hibiscus syrup, which pair wonderfully together and give a fresh, smooth quality to the cocktail.

Sloe to Get Up

1 oz. Bombay gin
1 oz. sloe gin
¾ oz. hibiscus syrup*
¾ oz. fresh lemon juice
Lemon twist (garnish)

*Hibiscus simple syrup   Combine 1 cup granulated sugar with 1 cup water in a saucepan. Heat over medium heat and stir frequently until sugar has been completely dissolved. Add 1 cup dried hibiscus flowers to the mixture, remove pan from heat, and let steep until flavor has been incorporated (thirty minutes to an hour).

<u>Here's How</u>   Combine all ingredients in a shaker with ice. Shake well and strain into a rocks glass with a one large cube. Garnish with lemon twist.

How 'Bout That!

• Tyson, the destroyer of men: Mike Tyson became the youngest heavyweight champion in the history of boxing after he defeated Trevor Berbick with a second round TKO; he was twenty years and four months old when it happened in November 1986.

• Tyson's mother died when he was only sixteen years old. He was left in care of boxing trainer and manager Cus D'Amato. By thirteen years of age, he'd been arrested thirty-eight times for petty crimes. Over the course of his boxing career, Tyson accrued more than $300 million, yet declared himself bankrupt in 2003.

• Hogan and the Terrible, Horrible, No Good Very Bad Decision: In 1994, Hulk Hogan got a call from his agent asking him if he'd be interested in endorsing what we now know as the George Foreman Grill . . . or, he had the choice of endorsing a meatball-making machine, not known by many as the Hulkamania Meatball Maker. The electric grill went on to sell more than one hundred million units and made Foreman over $200 million, more than he ever made slugging it out in the ring. As for Hogan, well, now he's left to wrestle with his decision for the rest of his life. Pun intended.

• Fighting for his life: Salamo Arouch was a Jewish boxer imprisoned at Auschwitz who was forced to fight other prisoners; the losers of the bouts were sent to the gas chambers or shot. Arouch survived over two years and two hundred fights. He was released when Auschwitz was liberated.

• As a child, Muhammad Ali was denied an autograph from his idol at the time, Sugar Ray Robinson. Sugar Ray's cold shoulder left a permanent mark on Ali, who vowed never to deny an autograph to fans, a promise he kept.

• Muhammad Ali and Joe Frazier met in the ring a total of three times. Who can forget their third fight in the Philippines, dubbed the Thrilla in Manila? Ali came out victorious after fourteen grueling rounds, a bout Ali said was "the closest thing to dying." He went on to add, "I'm so tired I want to rest for a week. My hips are sore, my arms are sore, my side is sore, my hands are sore."

• Props after a pummeling: Ali paid tribute to Frazier as "the toughest man in the world. I couldn't have taken the punches he took. I didn't realize he was so great. He's a real, real fighter."

- Ali went two months abstaining from sex, a feat he claimed made him unbeatable.
- Chess boxing, seriously? In Berlin and London, there's a growing sport called chess boxing, in which players alternate between a round of chess and boxing until someone is crowned the winner by checkmate, knockout, or technical stoppage. See, this is what happens when you ridicule a chess player one too many times.
- Bruce Lee's teacher, at least one of them, was a bad man and an illegal bare-knuckle champion who was undefeated for at least sixty fights. After accidentally blinding an opponent, he called it quits and retired.

Ultimate Fighting Championship (UFC)

It takes guts, and perhaps a little insanity, to enter the Octagon and fight in a UFC bout. But what many people may forget is just how much skill is required by these fighters, and these mixed martial artists are superbly trained and skilled at what they do. We see the culmination, the bloody conclusion of their months, sometimes years, of preparation. The UFC's popularity has skyrocketed in the past decade, but it was on the brink of going six feet under twenty years ago before it was rescued by two ultra-rich brothers. I created a drink to highlight the most identifiable element of the UFC, the arena in which battles take place, the Octagon, the eight-sided platform for UFC fans to marvel over. El Octagono uses eight different ingredients to create a powerful, citrusy cocktail to give you that warm buzz that only tequila can to get you ready for Fight Night.

El Octagono

½ oz. silver tequila
½ oz. reposado tequila
½ oz. añejo tequila
½ oz. mezcal
½ oz. Cointreau
¾ oz. lime juice
½ oz. simple syrup
Blood orange (wheels, for garnish)
Sanpellegrino Blood Orange Soda (to top)

<u>Here's How</u> Combine all ingredients except blood orange soda
in a mixing glass and shake well. Add blood orange wheels into a
highball glass. Strain into the highball glass and top with blood
orange soda.

How 'Bout That!

• Chuck Norris exerts his influence on yet another aspect of American culture; his 1980 ninja film, *The Octagon*, has become a cult hit among martial arts lovers and is likely the inspiration for the octagon ring shape UFC competitors battle in.

• A thin rule book: Pankration, the first real mixed martial art, was a combination of grappling and hand-to-hand combat invented by the ancient Greeks as a war strategy. However, the martial art was also played as an Olympic sport circa 648 BC. The only rules of Pankration: no biting, no eye gouging.

• Dirty, yet still shiny money: The UFC was about to fold in 2001 when it was bought for $2 million by the Fertitta brothers, who are believed to be heirs to a fortune built on organized crime. To further this assumption, UFC belts are made from real gold and cost $333,000 a pop. In 2016, the UFC resold for $4.2 billion . . . not a bad profit.

• Too violent for the Empire State: The UFC was deemed too brutal in the state of New York and on par with cockfighting in regards to the amount of blood and the fact that bouts didn't end until one contender was seriously injured. The state lifted the ban in 2016, likely when it realized how much money it was missing out on, as the amount of blood has not changed.

• Star-War-rior: George Lucas's daughter is a professional MMA fighter.

• Speak for yourself, Ali: Ronda Rousey, contradictory to Muhammad Ali, claims that a heavy dosage of sex before a match is good for female fighters because it boosts testosterone levels.

- Chomping at the bit: Those responsible for UFC 1 had the bright idea to have live alligators in a moat surrounding the Octagon.

- Mr. President, your class is about to begin: Dana White, UFC president, used to teach boxercise classes before coming to the UFC. He was also a boxer, but never went pro. It's safe to say he went in the right direction considering his net worth, as of 2019, is roughly $500 million.

- Holly Holm exploded in popularity after UFC 193, since she managed to dethrone one of the most dominant UFC Women's champions, Ronda Rousey. It was a clinical performance and domination, and Holms definitely deserved the win after her ferocious kick to the head knocked Rousey out cold in the second round. An especially sweet victory for Holms, who wasn't given much of a chance by the media.

- Bruce Buffer, the man known for calling "I-i-i-i-t's t-i-i-i-i-me!" and the ring announcer for the UFC, isn't just a pretty voice. He's a martial artist in his own right and holds a second-degree black belt in Tang Soo Do, a Korean martial art that is sometimes referred to as "Korean karate." Before becoming a ring announcer for the UFC, he was also a kick boxer but retired after suffering a concussion.

13
Rugby

RUGBY WORLD CUP

My introduction to rugby came from a close family friend, Richard, who had played all his life and gave me little tidbits about the game, such as what a scrum is, how points are scored, and a bit about the history of the game, including the most dominant country, New Zealand. I also remember him recounting his time spent with his rugby buddies; perhaps no sport has such a close-knit group of friends willing to party to no end and be there for one another should a teammate need help. There seems to be a devout loyalty to one another amongst rugby teammates.

It's no secret rugby players enjoy a drink now and again (now, and again and again) so I created a drink reflecting the toughness required to play. Black eyes, bruises, cuts, concussions—it's all part of the game, along with fellowship and drink.

Black-eyed Bourbon

2 oz. bourbon
½ oz. lemon juice
¾ oz. brown sugar simple syrup
1 oz. tart black cherry juice
4 thyme sprigs (divided)
Lemon twist (garnish)

<u>Here's How</u> Combine all ingredients, including 2 thyme sprigs, in a mixing glass. Fill with ice and shake well. Strain into a rocks glass with one large ice cube. Express a lemon twist over the drink then use as a garnish with remaining thyme.

How 'Bout That!

- Renaissance man: It's widely believed that the inventor of basketball, Dr. James Naismith, invented the game of rugby to keep his basketball players fit during the offseason.

- Twenty teams compete at the World Cup, and the same whistle is blown for the opening game of every Rugby World Cup tournament. The whistle was first used by a Welsh referee in 1905 during a game between New Zealand and England. Turns out the most dangerous part of rugby is not actually playing it, but blowing the bacteria-ridden whistle.

- The Rugby World Cup is played every four years, and the New Zealand All Blacks have won the Rugby World Cup three times: 1987, 2011, and 2015. The All Blacks, or ABs as they're commonly known, hold the record for most World Cup titles.

- Don't count the United States out. Rugby has been played in the Olympics only four times, the last coming in 1924, but of those four appearances, the United States is the most successful country, taking the gold in 1920 and 1924.

- The All Blacks of New Zealand dance the haka before the start of every match. In response to their dance, in 1905, the Welsh tried to match the All Blacks's ceremonial dance by breaking into song and singing the county's national anthem, "Hen Wlad Fy Nhadau," for the first time.

- Honey, I'll take out the trash if you can just help me blow up the balls: Modern rugby balls are made of high-tech materials that go through the full design process, but it wasn't always this way. Richard Lindon created the first-ever rugby balls using pigs' bladders covered in leather panels. But there was a problem: the valve and hand pump had not been invented yet, so Lindon's wife had the pleasure of blowing up the balls by mouth. Seems harmless, right? His wife paid the ultimate price after inhaling the air from too many diseased urine sacks. She came down with lung disease and died. Too much sports, literally, killed her.

14
Cycling

Tour de France

If you've ever ridden a bicycle, you can appreciate the extreme fitness required of the riders in the Tour de France as they peddle their way up the mountainsides of the some of the steepest grades in the French Alps. The race plays well on TV as commentators guide viewers across the French countryside with helicopter shots of imposing peaks and small villages scattered across the rolling hills. The tour has grown notorious for the volume of riders willing to cheat to capture the yellow jersey, which is unfortunate because the tour, and cycling fans, deserve better. The French people living in the countryside lead simple, fulfilling lives. Their existence is heightened by the "little" things of life—fresh bread and cheese, self-cultivated wine, friendship. Joie de Vivre!, or "Enjoyment of Life," is a cocktail that uses some of the best ingredients with French origins that hopefully inspire a joyful viewing experience of an extraordinary cycling event. Cheers!

Joie de Vivre!

1 oz. cognac
¾ oz. yellow chartreuse
½ oz. honey syrup*
½ oz. lemon juice
1 ½ oz. champagne
Lemon spiral (garnish)

*Honey syrup Combine equal parts honey and warm water and stir until combined.

Here's How Combine all ingredients, except champagne, in a mixing glass with ice. Shake well and strain into a coupe glass. Top with champagne and garnish with lemon spiral.

How 'Bout That!

- Takin' it to the streets: More than twelve million spectators line the route each year, making it the largest sporting event in the world.
- The winner of the tour receives $609,525 in cash, and tradition dictates that the winner split the money evenly with their teammates, who were mostly responsible for the winner wearing the yellow jersey at the conclusion of the race.
- Lie Strong: Lance Armstrong held the record for most Tour de France wins with seven, but he was stripped of those wins in 2012 for a multifaceted doping scandal involving blood transfusions and repeated denials on Armstrong's part. They say that "everything's bigger in Texas," and the Austin bike "legend" proved this in a big way with his epic fall from grace.
- The average cyclist burns seven thousand calories per stage during the tour. That's 123,900 calories for the entire race, or the equivalent of gorging on 252 McDonald's double cheeseburgers.
- Eddy Merckx and Mark Cavendish jointly hold the record for the most Tour de France stage wins with thirty-four.
- Booze Band-Aids: It wasn't until the 1960s when alcohol was banned from the tour. Forget the drunk fans running alongside the course, cyclists, up until the 1960s, drank alcohol during the race to numb the pain from the grueling stages. It was then banned because it was considered a stimulant.

• What goes up must come down: The 1947 winner of the tour, Jean Robic, was known for taking water bottles filled with lead on the stages to descend faster. Not sure he thought the plan through in terms of the weighted ascent.

• Smoke 'em if you got 'em! It's common knowledge that the health risks of smoking cigarettes were not always known. In the 1920s, smoking was actually thought to be beneficiary to riders, who would share cigarettes while riding, believing that smoking would "open their lungs up" for the big climbs.

• The tour is comprised of twenty to twenty-two competing teams, each with nine riders from around the world. Competitors can expect to cycle more than two thousand miles across France, up and down mammoth mountains and on routes that alternate between clockwise and counter-clockwise circuits of France.

• Rest? What rest? Rest days for riders in the Tour de France is not for lounging, as riders typically spend at least two hours on their bikes trying to flush out the built-up lactic acid in their legs.

• Sodden cyclist: Over the course of the two-thousand-mile tour, cyclists will sweat about 1.5 liters per hour, or thirty-two gallons over the course of the entire race. To put this number into perspective, it's enough sweat to flush a toilet more than twenty times, 1.6 gallons per flush.

• Deadly repercussions: Three riders have died while competing in the Tour de France, and another rider drowned during a rest day. In 1935, Francisco Cepeda, a Spaniard, had the unfortunate distinction of becoming the first rider to die after he lost control of his bike on the descent in the Alps of the infamous Col du Galibier as he crashed into a ravine.

• Why the yellow? The overall leader of the race gets to wear the yellow jersey, or maillot jaune, which was introduced into the tour in 1919. It's believed the yellow stemmed from a French newspaper and sponsor of the race that printed its publication on distinguishing yellow paper.

GIRO D'ITALIA

Although the lesser known of the major cycling events of the year—because it's not the Tour de France—the Giro d'Italia is an extremely formidable race. "Cima Coppi" means the highest elevation point in each Giro d'Italia, which is why I named the cocktail after this historical point on the course. My wife and I traveled to Cinque Terre in Italy on our honeymoon and were blown away by the size of the lemons we saw along a coastal hike. The lemons are abundant, and limoncello is served as an aperitif (before-dinner drink) or digestif (after-dinner drink). The Aperol spritz, which uses prosecco, is very popular in Italy, and I wanted to incorporate the prosecco into the cocktail to make Cima Coppi, an Italian cocktail at heart.

Cima Coppi

1 ½ oz. raspberry liqueur
1 oz. limoncello
2 ½ oz. prosecco
¼ oz. fresh lemon juice
Club soda (to top)
Raspberries (garnish)
Lemon twist (garnish)

<u>Here's How</u> In a cocktail glass, add the first four ingredients. Stir well and top with club soda. Garnish with raspberries and lemon twist on cocktail spear.

How 'Bout That!

- The Giro d'Italia was started by a local Italian newspaper, *La Gazzetta*, in an attempt to increase newspaper sales. The first race was held on May 13, 1909, and the main theme color of the Giro d'Italia is pink because the *Gazzetta* newspaper is, well, pink.
- The Giro d'Italia is broadcast to more than eight hundred million people in 174 countries and is considered as one of cycling's three major Grand Tours, along with the Tour de France in July and Vuelta a España in September.
- Not exactly an Italian vacation: The total elevation gain on all the thirty-nine categorized climbs is more than forty-four thousand meters, equal to going up Mount Everest four and a half times.
- The Cima Coppi is the highest altitude reached by cyclists during the Giro d'Italia. It was established in 1965 and named after cycling legend and previous Giro winner Fausto Coppi. The highest point of Cima Copi in history is Passo dello Stelvio (Stelvio Pass), which rises to 9,048 feet.

- Italian riders dominate the Giro d'Italia with the most Giro d'Italia wins (sixty-nine), followed by Belgian riders (seven) and Dutch riders (six).

- Peddlin' pretty in pink: The leader of the race wears the pink jersey called the maglia rosa. No one wears the maglia rosa on the first day, not even the previous year's winner. Eddy Merckx spent the most days in the maglia rosa with seventy-eight days.

- Each team fields 8 riders with a total of 176 riders. Every rider will have at least two road bikes and a time trial bike. Team leaders usually have three road bikes and two time trial bikes. There will be more than five hundred bikes at the Giro d'Italia and more than a thousand set of wheels.

- The overall Giro d'Italia winner is expected to pocket at least €205,668, but he doesn't keep it all to himself. Traditionally, the prize money is split among his teammates and the team's support staff. Each day in the maglia rosa—the race leader's pink jersey—nets the wearer a cool €1,000.

- The women's equivalent of the Giro d'Italia is the Giro Rosa, which started in 1988. In 1924, an Italian woman, Alfonsina Strada, took part in the Giro d'Italia when organizers mistook her as a male. She remains the only female to have ridden the Giro d'Italia.

- Even though the Giro d'Italia is an Italian cycling race, it doesn't always start in Italy. Since 1965, the Giro d'Italia has started outside of Italy thirteen times: San Marino (1965), Monaco (1966), Belgium (1973, 2006), Vatican City (1974), Greece (1996), France (1998), Netherlands (2002, 2010, 2016), Denmark (2012), Northern Ireland (2014), and Israel (2018).

- Bad in black: Between 1946 to 1951, there was maglia nera, or the black jersey. It was awarded to the rider who finished last in the Giro. It was then scrapped off to avoid riders deliberately wasting time just to win this jersey.

- The last rider to win the Giro d'Italia and Tour de France in the same year was Marco Pantani in 1998. Only ten riders in history have achieved a double Grand Tour win in a calendar year. Pantani was plagued by doping allegations and later died from a cocaine overdose.
- Cyclists need to eat six thousand to seven thousand calories per day to cope with the physical demands put on their bodies.

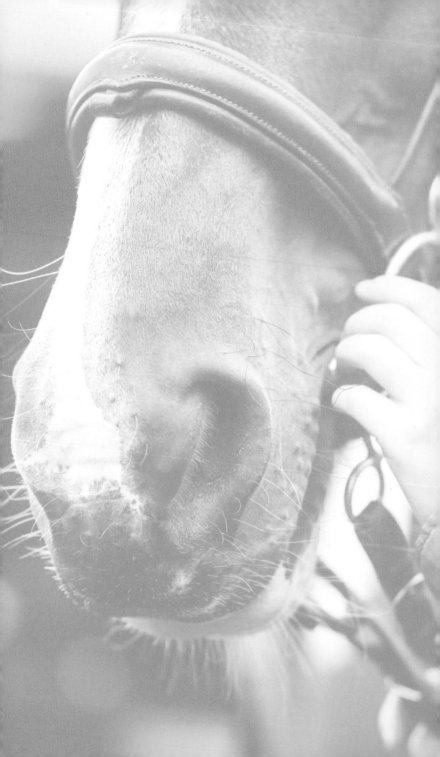

15
Horse Racing

Kentucky Derby

Get your best hats out because the derby is here! When people talk about horse racing, they talk about the Kentucky Derby—it's the definitive horse race that everyone's familiar with. The derby is the first leg of the American Triple Crown, the most coveted achievement in horse racing. The race is held in bourbon country—Louisville, Kentucky—and so it should come as no surprise that the mint julep, a simple cocktail made of bourbon, mint, and sugar, is the official drink of the derby and is nearly as famous as the two-minute race itself. The race is often called the Run for the Roses, as the winner is draped with a blanket of roses. I incorporated rose water to pay homage to this tradition, along with bourbon, since we are watching the spectacle take place in Kentucky. The basil and cantaloupe juice are my twist on the traditional julep, which again uses mint and sugar. "Riders up!" as the paddock judge traditionally commands for the jockeys to mount their horses for the race.

Basil Rose

2 oz. bourbon
1 ½ oz. fresh cantaloupe juice
10 basil leaves (divided, 2 for garnish)
3 dashes rose water

<u>Here's How</u> In a rocks glass, muddle the eight basil leaves to release the leaves' oils. Add crushed ice three-quarters the way up the glass. Add 3 dashes rose water, bourbon, and cantaloupe juice. Stir until outside of glass begins to frost. Add crushed ice to form a dome on top and garnish with two basil leaves.

How 'Bout That!

• The Kentucky Derby was started by Lewis Clark Jr., the grandson of William Clark, half of the famous explorer duo Lewis and Clark, after he saw England's Epsom Derby. When Clark founded the derby, he envisioned it as an event society's elite attended, just like races in Europe that required attendees to wear full morning dress. He used well-dressed, high-class folks to bring in his target audience for the first race, which worked. Eventually, the derby became a place to showcase the latest spring fashion. In the 1960s, women scrapped the more traditional outfits and branched out, which included wearing extravagant hats the Kentucky Derby is known for today.

- In 1919, Sir Barton became the first Triple Crown winner, even though he hadn't won a race before arriving at the derby.

- The Kentucky Derby is restricted to three-year-old thoroughbred horses and is exactly one mile and one-quarter long.

- The mint julep has been the traditional drink of the derby since 1938, and about 120,000 are served throughout the weekend to close to 160,000 attendees. That many juleps requires one thousand pounds of fresh mint, sixty thousand pounds of ice, and ten thousand bottles of Old Forester bourbon.

- Feel like your horse in the backyard has what it takes? The entry fee for a horse to run in the Kentucky Derby is $25,000.

- S is for serendipity: Nineteen past winners have had names beginning with the letter S, including Secretariat, the fastest horse in Kentucky Derby history, who completed the 1973 race in just under two minutes.

- Diane Crump was the first woman jockey ever to ride in the derby. There has yet to be a female winner, but Shelley Riley came the closest in 1992 when she finished in second.
- The purse for the 2019 derby was $3 million, with the winner taking home $1.86 million, $600,000 for second place, $300,000 for third place, $150,000 for fourth place, and $90,000 for fifth. From 2005 to 2018, the purse was "only" $2 million.
- The 2015 Kentucky Derby set a record with $194.3 million from total wagers on- and off-track.
- The race must go on: The derby has never been canceled or postponed due to inclement weather.
- The garland of roses presented to the winner is made up of more than four hundred roses, hence the term "Run for the Roses." The tradition of Run for the Roses originated in 1883 when New York socialite E. Berry Wall presented roses to ladies at a post-derby party that was attended by Churchill Downs founder and president, Colonel M. Lewis Clark. This gesture is believed to have led Clark to the idea of making the rose the race's official flower. The rose blanket weighs about forty pounds, and in the center of the garland is the rose "crown," with a single rose pointing up that symbolizes the heart and struggle needed to reach the Kentucky Derby Winner's Circle.
- Come on, ladies! Only three fillies have won the Kentucky Derby.

THE PREAKNESS STAKES

The second jewel of the Triple Crown, the Preakness is held at the Pimlico Race Course in Baltimore, Maryland. The Preakness and Belmont Stakes are often the forgotten of the "Big Three" races that make up the Triple Crown. The Preakness is held every year in Baltimore, Maryland, a city oozing with character, and not only from the soft-shell crab you just bit into. From their incredible National Aquarium, harbor, and the house and museum dedicated to claimed son and macabre poet Edgard Allan Poe, Baltimore has just about everything for anyone. I was interested to learn that the city actually has its own traditional drink, the lemon peppermint stick—basically an edible peppermint stick stuck into a halved lemon. The drink appears around Flower Mart, Mount Vernon's spring jubilee where guests wear garden hats and marvel at all the buds in bloom. I thought it would be appropriate to incorporate this tradition into the When Lemons Give You Life . . . cocktail as an ode to the Baltimore area and as a treat to enjoy when watching the Preakness at home.

When Lemons Give You Life . . .

1 oz. brandy
1 oz. limoncello
½ oz. Cointreau
2 ½ oz. fresh lemonade*
Club soda
Lemon wheel (garnish)
Peppermint leaves (garnish)

*Fresh lemonade Using handheld juicer, squeeze lemons to get 1 cup of lemon juice. Add 5 tablespoons of fine sugar. I use a mason jar for this and shake to combine until all sugar has dissolved. You can easily stir the mixture as well.

<u>Here's How</u> In a mixing glass, add the brandy, limoncello, Cointreau, and fresh lemonade. Shake well and strain into a Collins glass. Top with club soda and garnish with lemon wheel, peppermint leaves, and a red-and-white striped straw.

How 'Bout That!

• The Preakness Stakes is the second leg of the Triple Crown, the Kentucky Derby being the first, with the Belmont Stakes as the final test.

- Kentucky-bred: A total of ninety-seven Preakness winners have been bred in Kentucky. Maryland has bred eight, Florida seven, and Pennsylvania and California with six each. Eight Maryland breeds have won the Preakness.
- The Minisi, a northern New Jersey tribe of Native Americans, used to call their area Pra-qua-les, which meant "quail wood." The name eventually evolved into Preakness. A thoroughbred owner was attracted to the name in the 1870s, calling his farms in New Jersey and Kentucky "Preakness." His New Jersey farms were in the Native Americans' "quail woods." Preakness, New Jersey, remains there today.
- The favorite horse wins the Preakness more than half of the time. In 141 editions of the race, the favorite has emerged victorious 72 times.
- Since the turn of the century, seven of the sixteen Kentucky Derby winners have also won the Preakness. American Pharoah is the only one who completed the Triple at Belmont three weeks later.
- We know the Preakness as the second leg of the Triple Crown, but it was actually held before the Kentucky Derby eleven times between 1888 and 1931. Also, in 1890, the Preakness and the Belmont Stakes were both held on the same day.
- The winning owner is awarded the Woodlawn Vase, created by Tiffany & Co. The trophy is considered priceless. Not so. The trophy has an estimated appraised value of over $4 million, earning it the moniker of "the Most Valuable Trophy in American Sports."
- Forget the roses! A blanket of faux black-eyed Susans has been draped across the shoulders of the Preakness winner every year since 1940. The winner is draped in a blanket of Viking poms, which takes four people about eight hours to create. The blanket is made from daises and not black-eyed Susans, which are not in bloom until June in Maryland. The

daisies are daubed with black lacquer to recreate the appearance of the black-eyed Susan. The flower usually has thirteen petals, which symbolize the thirteen original colonies, including Maryland, and the flower represents the state's black and yellow colors.

THE BELMONT STAKES

The final chapter in every storied horses' book. The Triple Crown winner must capture the Belmont Stakes to be immortalized in big-time horse racing history. Like New York itself, a state bustling with change, the Belmont Stakes has had a number of "traditional changes" over the course of its life in Elmont, New York. My goal was to create a drink that captures the grandeur of possibility that is a horse actually capturing the Triple Crown. There is no state grander than New York, the Empire State, and no city more illustrious than New York City, the Big Apple, which is why I centered the cocktail around apple whiskey and dry hard cider. The Triple Crown is as an elusive achievement as they come—in fact, only thirteen thoroughbreds have lived the magic—amazing when you figure the three major races have been around for well over one hundred years. Why is the Triple Crown so difficult to win? The achievement requires horses to run three times in five weeks at three different tracks, all that vary in length, with the Belmont being the last, and longest, track.

The Crown Jewel

1 oz. Crown Royal Apple
1 oz. bourbon
½ oz. Heering Cherry Liqueur
½ oz. brown sugar simple syrup
¼ oz. fresh lemon juice
2 dashes black walnut bitters
Dry hard cider (to top)
3 slices fresh apple (garnish)

<u>Here's How</u> In a mixing glass, combine all ingredients except the cider. Shake well and strain into a coupe glass. Top with cider and garnish with apple slices.

How 'Bout That!

- The white carnation is the traditional flower of the Belmont Stakes, and the blanket of three hundred to four hundred carnations worn by the winner takes ten hours to put together. The flowers are shipped in from either California or Bogota, Colombia.
- The first stakes race and eventually the racetrack itself were named after August Belmont, who served as a prominent New York horseman and financier and as a pioneering chairman of the Jockey Club.
- The Belmont Stakes in Elmont, New York, is known as the Test of the Champion and the Run for the Carnations and has a reputation as the toughest test in the Triple Crown. The race is the longest, and last, race in the Triple Crown series. The Belmont is run on the largest dirt track in North America—Belmont Park—measuring a massive one and a half miles around. It's often said that this expansive layout makes the Churchill Downs and Pimlico Race Course one-mile ovals look like junior varsity tracks in comparison.
- In the early years of the Belmont, the race was run clockwise, as races are run in England, over a fishhook-shaped course, which included part of the current training track. The first counterclockwise Belmont Stakes was run in 1921.
- Horses that comprise the Belmont Stakes include three-year-old thoroughbred colts and geldings.
- A horse to remember: Secretariat ran the fastest time of 2:24:00 in 1973—a world record for one and a half miles on dirt. He also holds the world record for biggest win—thirty-

one lengths—on a one-and-a-half-mile track. The statue of Secretariat in the paddock at Belmont Park also receives a similar blanket of carnations to recognize his amazing performance in the 1973 Belmont Stakes.

• The iconic white pine tree in Belmont Park's paddock became Belmont Park's logo in 1968 and is estimated to be about two hundred years old.

• Props from the Empire: The Empire State Building has long recognized significant sporting events through the lighting of its spire, and green and white are the proud colors of the Belmont Stakes.

• Who needs ancient traditions anyways? Despite the fact the Belmont is the oldest of the three Triple Crown races, it isn't known for its longstanding traditions, mostly in part to the fact that its traditions have repeatedly changed throughout history. Quick examples: until 1996, the post parade song was "The Sidewalks of New York." In 1997, the song was changed to Frank Sinatra's "New York, New York." In an attempt to appeal to a younger audience, the song was once again changed in 2010 to Jay-Z's "Empire State of Mind" before quickly switching back to "New York, New York." When the trophy is presented, fans are encouraged to sing along to the theme from Martin Scorsese's 1977 film *New York, New York*. This is very similar to the singing of "Old Kentucky Home" at the Kentucky Derby and "Maryland, My Maryland" at the Preakness Stakes.

16
Cricket

ICC CRICKET WORLD CUP

Prior to creating *Sports Bar*, I'll admit that the sport of cricket was always something of a mystery to me. I remember flipping channels on the TV, landing on a station showing a cricket match, getting a quick laugh at the leg pads and bat, then continuing on my wave of channel surfing. Upon further review, I found that cricket is a fascinating game with a rich history dating back to the 1700s. I was shocked to learn how long cricket matches can last and wanted to create a drink using elements not only enjoyed across the globe, but a spirit capable of keeping you awake and alert should your favorite cricket-playing nation's match run up to the five-day maximum length, which was imposed after a particularly grueling match that went on for a record nine days!

Banana Espress

1 ½ oz. espresso vodka
1 oz. crème de cacao
½ oz. coconut milk
Ripe banana (1 quarter to be used for muddling)
Grated dark chocolate (for rim garnish)

<u>Here's How</u> In a mixing glass, muddle the banana quarter. Add remaining ingredients and ice and shake well. Moisten rim of coupe glass with coconut milk, then rim with dark chocolate

shavings. Strain into a coupe glass using a double strainer to catch any banana.

How 'Bout That!

- Sporting blasphemy: The first game of cricket ever to take place was in 1646. The game proved to be so popular that fines had to be given out to those sinners who played the game instead of attending church.
- When counting sheep loses its luster: Cricket is said to have originated in England with its shepherds who tended to their flocks. The grass was so short—because of the sheep—that it was possible to roll a lump of wool along it, which they used as a ball. The game was thought to have originated as a means of passing time among shepherds as they guarded their sheep.
- Baseball is America's premier bat-and-ball game, if not the most popular game in the country. But this wasn't always the case. Cricket was the first game ever to be played in the United States using a bat and ball. The game ruled the countryside between 1834 and 1914 with more than a thousand cricket clubs sprouting up across the forty-six states.
- Precious priorities: To protect their privates, male cricket players wear a cup, or "box," as it's commonly referred to in the cricket community. Gloves and a helmet accompany the box, and boxes were worn to protect men's genitals from the dawn of the game in the sixteenth century. Helmets weren't worn to protect their skulls until the 1970s—not exactly thinking outside of the "box" for quite some time, it seems.
- There are three forms of cricket: Test cricket, One Day International cricket, and Twenty20 cricket. The Cricket World Cup falls into the One Day International (ODI) cricket category. The most prestigious, not to mention the oldest, form of cricket is Test cricket, where matches last for a maxi-

mum of five days—this is playing daily from approximately 11:00 a.m. to 6:00 p.m. In this time period, bowlers (basically the pitchers of cricket) bowl ninety "overs" in a day, with two breaks for lunch and tea—again, no shock that the game was invented in England. If you're as confused as I was about what an over is, it's basically a series of six legal deliveries from the bowler to the batter.

• A game that knows no limits: Test matches originally had no time limit—the five-day limit mentioned above was put in place after an infamous match between South Africa and England in 1939. The game eventually had to be stopped after nine days of play—not because either team won, but because the England club would've missed their boat back to London. Due to logistics, there is no Test Cricket World Cup, since games can last up to five days.

• Only ten nations are allowed to play Test cricket, mostly former British Empire nations.

• Save some time, save the game: Twenty20 cricket was born in the mid-2000s, which is a form of the game lasting for twenty overs per team (again, overs being a series of six legal bowls). The Twenty20 cricket format allows for games to be finished in three hours. Many believe Twenty20 cricket has saved the game, as more and more people are interested—and able—to watch a game in its entirety.

• Down under dominance: Australia stands head and shoulders above the rest when it comes to World Cup titles. The nation has won the tournament on four occasions: 1987, 1999, 2003, and 2007.

SOURCES

GOLF

www.augusta.com/masters/photos/25-fun-facts-about-masters

Roadtrips.com, https://www.roadtrips.com/professional-golf-packages/masters/ultimate-itinerary/.

Owen, David. *The Making of the Masters.* New York: Simon & Schuster, 2003.

Reilly, Rick. *Who's Your Caddy?* New York: Doubleday, 2003.

Golficity.com, https://golficity.com/a-brief-history-of-the-ryder-cup/.

https://www.rydercup.com/news-media/usa/ryder-cup-golf-records-odd-accomplishments-and-facts

http://playtga.com/blog/2018/09/fun-facts-about-the-ryder-cup/

PGA Tour.com, https://www.pgatour.com/tournaments/ryder-cup.html.

https://sportycious.com/10-interesting-facts-ryder-cup-91717

https://www.golfdigest.com/gallery/british-open-facts-photos#14

https://www.britannica.com/sports/British-Open

https://www.golfdigest.com/gallery/photos-us-open-facts#12

https://www.cnn.com/2013/06/03/us/u-s-open-golf-tournament-fast-facts/index.html

https://www.liveabout.com/golfers-whose-only-tour-win-was-the-us-open-1565538

http://playtga.com/chc/2018/08/05/fun-facts-about-the-pga-championship/

https://www.pga.com/events/pgachampionship/11-surprising-facts-pga-championship

http://www.chiff.com/recreation/sports/pga-championship.htm

https://www.cnn.com/2013/06/05/us/pga-championship-fast-facts/index.html

HOCKEY

https://thehockeywriters.com/little-known-facts-about-the-stanley-cup/

http://mentalfloss.com/article/51140/22-things-you-might-not-know-about-stanley-cup

https://www.msgnetworks.com/2017/04/10/10-random-facts-about-the-stanley-cup-trophy/

http://mentalfloss.com/article/72084/9-facts-about-nhls-winter-classic

https://www.12up.com/posts/6257409-complete-history-of-the-nhl-winter-classic

https://wsbt.com/sports/notre-dame/crews-prepare-for-nhls-winter-classic
-inside-notre-dame-stadium

BASEBALL

https://www.history.com/tag/world-series
http://www.baberuthcentral.com/babesimpact/legends/the-curse-of-the
-bambino/
http://www.sportingnews.com/us/mlb/news/world-series-2016-cubs
-indians-curses-superstitions-billy-goat-rocky-colavito-red-sox
-bambino/1rb3s70058v8b13duq312tcaxv
https://bleacherreport.com/articles/375113-top-mlb-superstitions-and-rituals
https://www.mentalfloss.com/article/85076/15-major-facts-about-little
-league-baseball
https://www.mlb.com/cut4/mlb-players-who-played-in-llws-c145884558
http://mentalfloss.com/article/85076/15-major-facts-about-little-league
-baseball
https://www.newsday.com/sports/baseball/20-fun-facts-about-the-all-star
-game-1.3014575
https://www.history.com/this-day-in-history/major-league-baseballs-first
-all-star-game-is-held
https://www.ncaa.com/news/baseball/article/2019-06-26/here-are
-programs-most-college-world-series-titles
http://www.chiff.com/recreation/sports/college-world-series.htm
https://www.ncaa.com/news/baseball/article/2018-06-12/one-fact-you-may
-not-know-about-each-2018-college-world-series

TENNIS

Evan Evan's tours, https://evanevanstours.com/attractions/london
-attractions/wimbledon-lawn-tennis-museum-tickets/.
Huffpost.com, https://www.huffpost.com/entry/the-greatest-moment-in
-me_b_7299518.
Smithsonian magazine, https://www.smithsonianmag.com/history/a-brief
-history-of-wimbledon-156205892/.
https://www.active.com/tennis/articles/10-facts-to-know-as-you-watch-the
-u-s-open-tennis-championships
http://www.tenniscanada.com/news/infographic-14-cool-facts-about-the
-us-open/
https://ftw.usatoday.com/2018/08/us-open-tennis-facts-records-stats
-federer-serena-money-50
https://sportycious.com/10-important-facts-french-open-like-know-9621
https://www.cnn.com/2013/06/03/world/europe/french-open-fast-facts
/index.html

https://ftw.usatoday.com/2017/05/french-open-2017-roland-garros-why-red
-clay-fun-facts-did-you-know-photos
http://swim.by/interesting-facts-about-australian-open-melbourne/
https://www.msn.com/en-au/sport/tennis/the-major-down-under-15
-interesting-facts-about-the-australian-open/ss-BBIgc4V
https://www.sportskeeda.com/tennis/10-lesser-known-facts-about-the
-australian-open/10

Soccer

https://www.nation.co.ke/sports/football/Interesting-facts-about-the-Fifa
-World-Cup/1102-4321694-rgw8k6z/index.html
https://www.mantelligence.com/17-world-cup-facts-you-dont-know/
https://www.sporcle.com/blog/2018/05/18-random-facts-about-the-world
-cup/
https://timesofindia.indiatimes.com/sports/football/fifa-world-cup/fun
-facts-about-fifa-world-cup-every-football-fan-should-know
/articleshow/64584485.cms
https://www.sportskeeda.com/football/copa-america-2016-7-interesting
-facts-about-tournament/7
http://copaamericalive.com/some-interesting-facts-of-copa-america/
https://www.britannica.com/sports/Copa-America
https://www.uefa.com/uefachampionsleague/news/newsid=2038584.html
https://www.uselessdaily.com/sports/uefa-champions-league-trivia-28-facts
-you-didnt-know/#ixzz5xAZsjyPY

Football

https://www.thisisinsider.com/facts-about-the-super-bowl-2018-2#a-lot-of
-thought-goes-into-the-super-bowl-location-and-the-venue-is
-determined-way-in-advance-12
https://www.rd.com/culture/super-bowl-facts/
https://www.newsday.com/sports/football/super-bowl/super-bowl-fun-facts
-1.6724231
https://www.profootballhof.com/news/vince-lombardi-trophy/
https://worldstrides.com/blog/2018/12/interesting-facts-about-college-bowl
-games/
https://www.cnn.com/2014/08/14/us/college-football-playoff-fast-facts
/index.html
https://www.footballbabble.com/football/college/facts/
https://ftw.usatoday.com/2018/03/nfl-draft-facts
https://www.sportingnews.com/us/nfl/news/how-does-the-nfl-draft-work
-rules-rounds-eligibility-and-more/0431yshpol431e7543pcrzpg1
http://www.nfl.com/draft/t

Auto Racing

https://thenewswheel.com/10-fun-facts-about-the-daytona-500-you-might
-not-know/

https://www.daytonainternationalspeedway.com/Articles/2016/04/Top
-10-Little-Known-Facts.aspx

http://blog.itrip.net/13-fast-facts-about-daytona-international-speedway/

https://www.chicagotribune.com/sns-daytonatrack-facts-story.html

https://racingnews.co/2017/09/21/nascar-sponsorship-costs/

http://thebrushback.com/daytona_full.htm

https://www.newsday.com/sports/motor-racing/20-fun-facts-about-the
-indy-500-1.2910256

https://www.history.com/this-day-in-history/first-indianapolis-500-held

http://mentalfloss.com/article/27852/10-mostly-obscure-indy-500-facts
-sure-impress-your-friends-least-slow-lane-kind-day

https://theculturetrip.com/europe/monaco/articles/11-fascinating-facts-to
-know-about-the-monaco-grand-prix/

https://social.f1experiences.com/monaco-grand-prix-fast-facts

https://luxurylaunches.com/other_stuff/interesting-facts-monaco-grand
-prix.php/2/

Action Sports

https://www.britannica.com/sports/Alpine-skiing

https://www.reuters.com/article/olympics-alpine-skiing-factbox/factbox
-olympics-alpine-skiing-interesting-facts-idUSLDE61A2W120100212

http://justfunfacts.com/interesting-facts-about-skiing/

https://www.telegraph.co.uk/travel/ski/galleries/10-greatest-World-Cup
-ski-racers

https://www.redbull.com/in-en/red-bull-rampage-essential-info

https://www.esquire.com/lifestyle/a14027508/red-bull-rampage-2017
-extreme-mountain-biking/

https://www.factmonster.com/sports/miscellaneous-sports/x-games

https://cliffdiving.redbull.com/m/en_US

https://www.swimmersdaily.com/2019/08/10/12-facts-you-didnt-know
-about-red-bull-cliff-diving/

https://www.xgamesmediakit.com/read-me

https://www.factmonster.com/sports/miscellaneous-sports/x-games

https://www.espn.com/action/xgames/winter/2011/news/story?page=2011
-winter-x-games-feats

Basketball

https://clutchpoints.com/24-interesting-facts-about-the-nba-finals/

https://study.com/blog/fun-facts-about-basketball-to-know-before-the-nba
-finals-start.html

https://bleacherreport.com/articles/1095524-50-random-nba-facts-you-never
-knew#slide49

http://wearebasket.net/players-with-the-most-nba-championships/

https://www.foxsports.com/southwest/gallery/21-fun-facts-about-march
-madness-031814

https://www.sportingnews.com/us/ncaa-basketball/list/ncaa-tournament
-2017-march-madness-bracket-ucla-duke-north-carolina-kansas
/vmxrvl8vnxmg13ukcvx4b4cnd

https://www.usnews.com/news/slideshows/7-mad-facts-about-march
-madness?slide=8

https://www.cnn.com/2013/09/06/us/nba-all-star-game-fast-facts/index
.html

http://www.chiff.com/recreation/sports/nba-all-star-game.htm

https://www.sportingnews.com/us/nba/news/nba-slam-dunk-contest
-history-past-winners-participants-all-time-great-moments
/183spw7b23jx11n4kz892c54pm

Combat Sports

http://www.funtrivia.com/en/Sports/Heavyweight-Division-5788_2.html

http://news.bbc.co.uk/onthisday/hi/dates/stories/october/1/newsid
_4074000/4074712.stm

https://www.kickassfacts.com/25-kickass-and-interesting-facts-about
-boxing/

https://www.thesun.co.uk/sport/wwe/2181483/how-the-george-foreman
-grill-was-merely-minutes-away-from-becoming-forever-known-as
-the-hulk-hogan-grill/

What culture.com, https://whatculture.com/topic/ultimate-fighting
-championship.

https://bleacherreport.com/articles/1008571-50-random-mma-facts-you
-never-knew#slide28

https://www.tvovermind.com/17-interesting-facts-mma-ufc/

Rugby

https://www.radionz.co.nz/news/sport/365914/rugby-world-cup-the-facts

https://www.squizzes.com/rugby-world-cup-facts/

https://www.teamsontour.com/the-dugout/2015/09/10-amazing-rugby
-facts/

https://www.gizmodo.co.uk/2015/09/10-facts-you-might-not-know-about
-the-game-of-rugby/

CYCLING

https://www.active.com/cycling/articles/23-fun-facts-you-didn-t-know
-about-the-tour-de-france

https://www.annieandre.com/tour-de-france-facts/

https://www.cnn.com/2013/06/05/world/europe/tour-de-france-fast-facts
/index.html

https://www.thegeekycyclist.com/pro-cycling/giro-d-italia-facts/

https://www.independent.ie/sport/other-sports/25-facts-about-the-giro
-ditalia-30260212.html

https://cycling-passion.com/cima-coppi/

HORSE RACING

https://www.equestrianstylist.com/equestrian-events/11-fun-facts-about
-the-kentucky-derby/

https://www.townandcountrymag.com/leisure/sporting/news/a2857
/kentucky-derby-facts/

https://www.rd.com/culture/kentucky-derby-facts/

https://www.wbaltv.com/article/13-fun-facts-about-the-preakness-stakes
/9867084

https://www.americasbestracing.net/lifestyle/2017-eleven-fun-facts-the
-preakness-stakes

https://www.betfirm.com/preakness-stakes-trivia/

https://www.newsday.com/sports/horseracing/belmont-stakes/17-fun-facts
-about-the-belmont-stakes-1.3750386

https://www.betfirm.com/belmont-stakes-facts/

https://www.americasbestracing.net/lifestyle/2014-ten-fun-facts-about-the
-belmont-stakes

https://www.nydailynews.com/sports/more-sports/belmont-15-fun-facts
-horse-racing-spotlight-turns-ny-article-1.2668616

CRICKET

http://www.sportabroad.co.uk/interesting-cricket-facts/

http://www.10-facts-about.com/cricket/id/72

https://deadspin.com/the-complete-guide-to-understanding-cricket
-1788456326

Bryan Paiement grew up in Roanoke, Virginia. Sports have always been a huge part of his life thanks to his French-Canadian father, who came to Virginia to play hockey for a minor league club and instilled a passion in him for sports of all kinds. Years later, after starting a small garden with his wife, Dana, he discovered a love for mixing cocktails using fresh ingredients such as basil, cantaloupe, and thyme, to name a few.